Society American Tract

**Hymns of Happy Voices**

Society American Tract

**Hymns of Happy Voices**

ISBN/EAN: 9783744737951

Printed in Europe, USA, Canada, Australia, Japan

Cover: Foto ©Thomas Meinert / pixelio.de

More available books at **www.hansebooks.com**

# THE
# HYMNS

OF

# "HAPPY VOICES,"

WITHOUT THE MUSIC.

AMERICAN TRACT SOCIETY,

150 NASSAU-STREET, NEW YORK.

# HYMNS

## OF

# HAPPY VOICES.

————•————

### 1.  The Happy Land.

1. THERE is a happy land,
    Far, far away,
   Where saints in glory stand,
    Bright, bright as day.
   Oh, how they sweetly sing,
   "Worthy is our Saviour King;"
   Loud let his praises ring,
    Praise, praise for aye.

2. Come to that happy land,
    Come, come away.
   Why will ye doubting stand,
    Why still delay?
   Oh, we shall happy be
   When from sin and sorrow free,
   Lord, we shall dwell with thee,
    Blest, blest for aye.

3

3. Bright, in that happy land,
     Beams every eye :
   Kept by a Father's hand;
     Love cannot die.
   Oh, then to glory run
   Be a crown and kingdom won ;
   And bright, above the sun,
     We'll reign for aye.

## 2.   Happy Voices.

1. NATURE's cheerful voices
All in harmony chime :
Songs from the trees, songs o'er the seas,
Murmurs soft on the floating breeze,
     Songs, best of all,
Of childhood's merry time.

CHORUS.          ·

Thus then your powers employ,
Happy voices, full of life and joy,
Gladness and love,
Learning melodies for the world above.

2. All things praise their Maker,
   Each with a different voice ;
Some to the eye praise silently,
Like yon stars in the evening sky ;
     But sons of God
   With heart and soul rejoice. —CHORUS.
4

3. Cold and dull were Eden's
Groves and murmuring rills,
Till high in air burst on the ear
Warbling notes of the lark, full and clear.
Life, life alone
The living bosom thrills.

4. Cold and dead the world lies,
E'en with its myriad songs,
Till here and there rise on the air
Praises pure, and believing prayer,
Soaring to God
Amid the angelic throngs.

5. Not like stars nor birds then,
Praise we the heavenly King;
With song and lyre, anthem and choir,
Hands that, working for Christ, never tire,
And hearts of love,
Whence all good thoughts do spring.

———————◆———————

## 8. Awake, and Sing the Song. S. M.

1. AWAKE, and sing the song
Of Moses and the Lamb;
Wake, every heart and every tongue,
To praise the Saviour's name.

5

2. Sing of his dying love,
   Sing of his rising power,
  Sing how he intercedes above
   For those whose sins he bore.

3. Sing till we feel our heart
   Ascending with our tongue;
  Sing till the love of sin depart,
   And grace inspire our song.

4. Sing on your heavenly way,
   Ye ransomed sinners, sing;
  Sing on, rejoicing every day
   In Christ the eternal King.

5. Soon shall we hear him say,
   "Ye blessèd children, come;
  Soon will he call us hence away,
   And take his wanderers home.

6. Soon shall our raptured tongue
   His endless praise proclaim,
  And sweeter voices tune the song
   "Of Moses and the Lamb."  HAMM'

## 4. Flowers, Sweet Flowers.

1. How sweet are the flowers
Of the garden and field,
When earth wears her summer array;
  6

How laden the air
With the fragrance they yield,
How varied the hues they display.
CHORUS.
Flowers of the wild-wood,
Flowers of the garden,
Emblems of childhood,
Flowers, sweet flowers.

2. But frail is their texture
And transient their stay,
For brief is the life of a flower;
Their fragrance and beauty
Too soon pass away,
They gladden the heart for an hour.
CHORUS—Flowers of the wild-wood, etc.

3. Some, plucked by the hand
Of the envious or rude,
Their life and their loveliness yield;
While some by the pitiless
Mower are strewed,
To wither like grass of the field.

4. Thus fair are the children
In home's sunny ground,
Thus frail as the floweret are they;
The scythe of the mower
Is sweeping around,
They're fading and passing away.

7

5. We 'll give them our prayers
And the heart-cheering word;
Thus nurtured by sunshine and shower,
Their virtues may scatter
A fragrance around
Surviving the fall of the flower.
Chorus—Flowers of the wild-wood, etc.
REV. A. A. GRALEY.

---

## 5. Won't You Volunteer?

1. Come, boys. come, girls,
Wo n't you volunteer?
If you 'd reign in heaven above,
You must battle here;
Say not, say not,
We are weak and few;
Only battle for the right,
God will strengthen you.

### CHORUS.

March on, march on, singing as you go;
March on, march on, do not fear the foe.

2. Come, boys, come. girls,
Wo n't you volunteer?
Youthful soldiers of the cross,
To our ranks repair:

8

List not, list not,
   To the world and sin,
Turn away from foes without,
   And from foes within.
      CHORUS—March on, march on, etc.

3. Come, boys, come, girls,
   Wo n't you volunteer?
Jesus bought you with his blood;
   How can you forbear?
Sinful, dying,
   To your help he flew:
Wo n't you love and live for him
   Who has died for you?

4. Come, boys, come, girls,
   Wo n't you volunteer?
Soon the vict'ry shall be yours,
   If you persevere:
Singing, shining,
   On a heavenly throne,
You shall strike a harp of gold
   And wear a golden crown.

## 6. Morning Bells.

1. HARK, the morning bells are ringing!
   Children, haste without delay;
Prayers of thousands now are winging
   Up to heaven their silent way.

9

CHORUS.

Come, children, come, the bells are ringing,
To the school with haste repair;
Let us all unite in singing,
All unite in solemn prayer.

2. 'T is an hour of happy meeting,
Children meet for praise and prayer;
But the hour is short and fleeting,
Let us then be early there.
CHORUS—Come, children, come, etc.

3. Do not keep our teachers waiting,
While you tarry by the way;
Nor disturb the school reciting,
'T is the holy Sabbath-day.

4. Children, haste, the bells are ringing,
And the morning's bright and fair;
Thousands now unite in singing,
Thousands too in solemn prayer.

---

### 7.   Infant Choir.

1. WHO shall sing if not the children?
Did not Jesus die for them?
May they not, with other jewels,
Sparkle in his diadem?

10

Why to them were voices given—
  Bird-like voices, sweet and clear?
Why, unless the songs of heaven
  They begin to practise here?

2. There's a choir of infant songsters,
    White-robed, round the Saviour's throne,
  Angels cease, and waiting listen:
    Oh, 't is sweeter than their own.
  Faith can hear the rapturous choral,
    When her ear is upward turned;
  Is not this the same perfected
    Which upon the earth they learned?

3. Jesus, when on earth sojourning,
    Loved them with a wondrous love;
  And will he, to heaven returning,
    Faithless to his blessing prove?
  Oh, they cannot sing too early:
    Fathers, stand not in their way.
  Birds do sing while day is breaking:
    Tell me then why should not they?

---

## 8.  Birth of Christ.

1. HARK, what mean those holy voices
    Sweet sounding through the skies?
  Lo, th' angelic host rejoices,
    Heavenly hallelujahs rise.

11

CHORUS.

Hear them tell the wondrous story,
  Hear them chant in hymns of joy,
"Glory, glory, glory, glory!
  Glory in the highest, glory!
Glory, glory, glory, glory!
  Glory be to God most high!"

2. "Peace on earth, good will from heaven,
  Reaching far as man is found;
Souls redeemed and sins forgiven,"
  Loud their golden harps shall sound.
    CHORUS—Hear them tell, etc.

3. "Christ is born, the great Anointed,
  Heaven and earth his praises sing;
Oh receive whom God appointed
  For your Prophet, Priest, and King."

4. "Hasten, mortals, to adore him,
  Learn his name and taste his joy;
Till in heaven ye sing before him,
  Glory be to God most high!"

————•————

## 9.  Praise to God.

1. PRAISE to God the great Creator;
  Praise to God from every tongue
Join, my soul, with every creature,
  Join the universal song.
  12

Father, source of all compassion,
    Pure, unbounded grace is thine ;
Hail the God of our salvation !
    Praise him for his love divine

2. Joyfully on earth adore him,
    Till in heaven our song we raise ;
Then, enraptured, fall before him,
    Lost in wonder, love, and praise :
Praise to God the great Creator,
    Father, Son, and Holy Ghost ;
Praise him, every living creature,
    Earth and heaven's united host.

                  FAWCETT.

## 10. Now is the Time.

1. BELIEVE it, dear children,
    That now is the time
To turn from the pathway
    Of folly and crime ;
To enter the way
    Which the ransomed have trod,
The way which leads upward
    To glory and God.

### CHORUS.

Now is the time, now is the time ;
Believe it, dear children, that now is the time.

2. But if you inquire
   Why the future won't do
As well as the present
   That way to pursue
Remember that death
   Hovers over your path,
And over you gathers
   A tempest of wrath.
      CHORUS—Now is the time, etc.
         .

3. But should you be spared
   E'en to threescore and ten,
Each year full of sorrow
   And shame will have been;
And what have you gained
   By this guilty delay?
A heart less inclined
   To believe and obey.

4. Don't say, "When religion
   Possesses the soul,
All cheerfulness withers
   Beneath its control."
Religion and happiness
   Ever combine;
But shame and remorse
   Are the wages of sin.
14

5. Then now is the time
   To secure the "good part,"
That sanctifies while
   It rejoices the heart;
The day of acceptance
   Is passing away;
Then haste to the Saviour,
   Dear children, to-day.    A. A. G.

---

## 11. Around the Throne.

1. AROUND the throne of God in heaven
   Thousands of children stand;
Children whose sins are all forgiven,
   A holy, happy band,
      Singing "Glory, glory,
      Glory be to God on high."

2. In flowing robes of spotless white
   See every one arrayed;
Dwelling in everlasting light,
   And joys that never fade,
      Singing, Glory, glory, glory, etc.

3. What brought them to that world above,
   That heaven so bright and fair,
Where all is peace and joy and love?
   How came those children there?
      Singing, Glory, glory, glory, etc.
15

4. Because the Saviour shed his blood
    To wash away their sin :
  Bathed in that pure and precious flood,
    Behold them white and clean,
        Singing, Glory, glory, glory, etc.

5. On earth they sought the Saviour's grace,
    On earth they loved his name ;
  So now they see his blessed face,
    And stand before the Lamb,
        Singing, Glory, glory, glory, etc.

### 12.  Universal Praise.

1. THE valleys and the mountains
    The woodland and the plain,
  The rivers and the fountains,
    The sunshine and the rain,
  The stars that shine above me,
    The flowers that deck the sod,
Proclaim aloud the glory of my God.
  Praises, holy adoration,
    Praises to the God above ;
  Praises through the wide creation,
    Sound aloud his greatness and his love.

2. And shall the voice of nature
    Thus glorify its King ;
  And man, the noble creature,
    No grateful tribute bring ?
    16

Shall mercy strew his pathway,
　And all the senses please,
And man withhold the sacrifice of praise?
　Praise him, ye that live for ever;
　　Praise him every heart and voice;
　Praise him, he's the glorious Giver;
　　Praise him in your sorrows and your joys


3. The word of life he gave us
　　To guide us to the sky;
　That he might justly save us,
　　He sent his Son to die—
　To die in shame and anguish,
　　To die a sacrifice;
To save us from the death that never dies.
　Praise him, praise him for salvation;
　　Praise him, praise him for his Son;
　Praise him, every tribe and nation;
　　Praise him for the battle he has won.


4. Then train your youthful voices
　　To hymn his praise above;
　For he who here rejoices
　　In Jesus' dying love,
　Around his throne in glory
　　Shall all his love proclaim,
And sing the song of Moses and the Lamb.

Praise him, praise the eternal Father ;
Praise him, praise the eternal Son ;
Praise him, praise the Three together,
Father, Son, and Spirit, three in One.

A. A. G

---

### 13. To Thee, my God and Saviour.

1. To thee, my God and Saviour,
   My heart exulting springs,
   Rejoicing in thy favor,
   Almighty King of kings :
   I 'll celebrate thy glory
   With all the saints above,
   And tell the wondrous story
   Of thy love.

#### CHORUS.

Glory! glory, hallelujah !
   Glory to the God of love ;
Glory! glory, hallelujah !
   Glory ever be to God above

2. Soon as the morn with roses
   Bedecks the dewy east,
   And when the sun reposes
   Upon the ocean's breast,

18

My voice in supplication,
　Jehovah, thou shalt hear ;
Oh grant me thy salvation,
　And draw near.
　　Chorus—Glory, glory, etc.


3. By thee, through life supported,
　I pass the dangerous road,
By heavenly hosts escorted
　Up to their bright abode ;
There cast my crown before thee,
　My toils and conflicts o'er,
And gratefully adore thee
　　Evermore.
　　Chorus—Glory, glory, etc.

---

## 14. Hosanna.

1. What are those soul-reviving strains,
Which echo thus from Salem's plains ?
What anthems loud, and louder still,
So sweetly sound from Zion's hill ?

### CHORUS.

'Glory, glory !" let us sing,
While heaven and earth with "Glory !" ring :
Hosanna, hosanna, hosanna to the Lamb of God

2. Lo, 't is an infant chorus sings
   "Hosanna to the King of kings!"
   The Saviour comes, and babes proclaim
   Salvation sent in Jesus' name.

3. Messiah's name shall joy impart
   Alike to Jew and Gentile heart:
   He bled for us, he bled for you,
   And we will sing Hosanna too.

4. Proclaim hosannas loud and clear;
   See David's Son and Lord appear:
   All praise on earth to him be given,
   And "Glory!" shout through highest heaven.

## 15. The Fountain.

1. Oн, there is a fountain
      That never is dry,
   The wounds of L manuel
      That fountain supply:
   From ages to ages
      The crimson stream flows,
   ||:To cleanse the polluted
      And lighten their woes.:||

2. 'T s there in his childhood
      A sinner may go,
   And manhood may wash
      Till he's whiter than snow;
   20

And age, by his sins
　And his sorrows oppressed,
||:May find in the wounds
　Of the Saviour a rest. :||

3. No vileness too vile
　For that fount to remove,
No sinner too sinful
　Its virtues to prove ;
If conscience reproaches,
　If terrors appal,
||:'T was opened for you,
　For 't was opened for all. :||

4. Then come to the fountain
　So gushing and red ;
A tempest of wrath
　Mutters over your head,
And the moments of mercy
　Are passing away :
||:Then come to the fountain,
　Poor sinner, to-day. :||　　　▲ ▲ ●

---

## 16.　Hallelujah.

1. In the far better land
　Of glory and light
The ransomed are singing
　In garments of white,

The harpers are harping,
　And all the bright train
Sing the song of redemption—
　"The Lamb that was slain."

CHORUS.

Hallelujah to the Lamb,
Hallelujah to the Lamb,
Hallelujah, hallelujah,
Hallelujah, Amen.

2. Like the sound of the sea
　Swells the chorus of praise
Round the star-circled crown
　Of the Ancient of days,
And thrones and dominions
　Reëcho the strain
Of glory eternal
　To Him that was slain.
CHORUS—Hallelujah to the Lamb  etc.

3. Dear Saviour, may we,
　With our voices so faint,
Sing the chorus celestial
　With angel and saint?
Yes, yes, we will sing,
　And thine ear we will gain
With the song of redemption—
　"The Lamb that was slain."
22

4. Now, children and teachers
   And friends, all unite
In a loud hallelujah
   With the ransomed in light;
To Jesus we'll sing
   That melodious strain,
The song of redemption—
   "The Lamb that was slain."
E. S. PORTER, D.

## 17. Life a Race.

1. THIS life is a race,
   And brief is the space
In which the great prize must be won:
   Then do not delay,
   For happy are they
Who early determine to run.

CHORUS.

Run in the race, run in the race,
Run in the race for glory.

2. At once then begin,
   Cast off every sin
And weight that encumbers the soul;
   And enter the track
   And never look back,
Till safely arrived at the goal.

CHORUS—Run in the race, etc.

3. When faint and oppressed,
   Some foe may suggest,
" 'T were better the race to give o'er ; ''
   But do not sit down ;
   Just think of the crown,
And that will revive you once more.


4. Yes, think of the crown,
   And let the world frown,
'T is better by far than its smile :
   It shall not destroy ;
   And as for its joy,
It only allures to defile.


5. Awake then, arise!
   Contend for the prize ;
What glories around it are flung :
   Oh fly from the path
   That leads down to wrath,
And run for the crown while you 're young.

A. A. G.

---

## 18.  Come and Join the Army.

1. WE 'RE marching to the camp above ;
   Oh wo n't you come and join us?
We 've shaken off the chains of sin,
   No longer they confine us ;
24

CHORUS.

Then come and join the army,
Then come and join the army ;
Oh gird the gospel armor on,
And come and join the army.

2. We once as rebels boldly fought,
    The rebel banner o'er us ;
But Jesus won us by his cross,
    And now leads on before us.
        CHORUS—Then come and join, etc.

3. And though against the shield of faith
    The fiery darts may rattle,
A soldier Jesus never lost,
    And never lost a battle.

4. He 'll give us peace and holy joy
    On this side of the river,
And when we've passed the swelling flood,
    Eternal life for ever.

5. And soon the conflict will be o'er ;
    And will it not be glorious
To leave the battle-field for heaven,
    Rejoicing and victorious !

A. A. G.

## 19. Will You Go?

1. WE 'RE travelling home to heaven above ;
        Will you go?  Will you go?
To sing the Saviour's dying love ;
        Will you go?  Will you go?
Millions have reached that blest abode,
Anointed kings and priests to God ;
And millions more are on the road,
        Will you go?  Will you go?

2. We 're going to walk the plains of light ;
        Will you go?  Will you go?
Far, far from curse and death and night ;
        Will you go?  Will you go?
The crown of life we then shall wear,
The conqueror's palm we then shall bear,
And all the joys of heaven we 'll share ;
        Will you go?  Will you go?

3. The way to heaven is straight and plain ;
        Will you go?  Will you go?
Repent, believe, be born again ;
        Will you go?  Will you go?
The Saviour cries aloud to thee,
"Take up thy cross and follow me,
And thou shalt my salvation see."
        Will you go?  Will you go?

4. Oh, could I hear some sinner say,
   "I will go, I will go."
Oh, could I hear him humbly pray,
   "Make me go, Make me go;"
And all his old companions tell,
"I will not go with you to hell,
I long with Jesus Christ to dwell;
   Let me go, Let me go.

## 20. Little Pilgrims.

1. THE way to heaven is narrow,
   And its blessed entrance strait;
But how safe the little pilgrims
Who get within the gate!

### CHORUS.

And we may join the pilgrim band
That journeys towards the light,
For the golden gate of that happy land
Stands open day and night.

2. The sunbeams of the morning
   Make the narrow pathway fair,
And these early little pilgrims
   Find dewy blessings there.
      CHORUS—And we may join, etc.

3. They pass o'er rugged mountains,
    But they climb them with a song;
For these early little pilgrims
    Have sandals new and strong.

4. They do not greatly tremble,
    When the shadows night foretell;
For these early little pilgrims
    Have tried the path full well.

5. They know it leads to heaven,
    With its bright and open gates,
Where for happy little pilgrims
    A Saviour's welcome waits.

REV. C. C. CARPENTER.

## 21. When We are Twenty-one.

1. WHEN we are twenty-one, boys,
    When we are twenty-one,
We cast the fetters off, boys,
    Our pupilage is done;
Before us is the world, boys,
    We'll try what it can do;
||:It promises so fair, boys,
    We'll prove it false or true. :||

2. There is a ruby cup, boys;
    'T is held in Pleasure's hand;
We'll quaff it long and deep, boys,
    A happy, jovial band;

And treasure we 'll secure, boys,
    And honor's steep we 'll climb,
||:And sober thoughts we 'll leave, boys,
    To those who 've passed their prime. :||


3. But hark! I hear a voice, boys;
    It whispers, "Youth, beware!
Before you 're twenty-one, boys,
    The dream may disappear—
The blooming cheek grow pale, boys,
    And dim the sparkling eye,
||:And in death's cold embrace, boys,
    The active form may lie. :||


4. "Talk not of twenty-one, boys,
    Talk not of twenty-one;
The present *now* is all, boys,
    That you can call your own;
Each moment as it glides, boys,
    Its hidden store reveals;
||:But who can pierce the veil, boys
    Which future years conceals?:||


5. "'T were madness then to sing, boys,
    And boast of years to come;
Awake from folly's dream, boys,
    The Saviour calls you home;

Now while the harvest waves, boys,
    The reaper's garb put on,
||:And gather sheaves for heaven, boys.
    Before you 're twenty-one.":||   ▲ ▲ ▲

---

### 22.  I Want to be an Angel.

1. I WANT to be an angel,
    And with the angels stand,
A crown upon my forehead,
    A harp within my hand;
There, right before my Saviour,
    So glorious and so bright,
I'd wake the sweetest music,
    And praise him day and night.

2. I never should be weary,
    Nor ever shed a tear,
Nor ever know a sorrow,
    Nor ever feel a fear;
But blessed, pure, and holy,
    I'd dwell in Jesus' sight,
And with ten thousand thousands
    Praise him both day and night.

3. I know I'm weak and sinful,
    But Jesus will forgive;
For many little children
    Have gone to heaven to live.

Dear Saviour, when I languish,
　　And lay me down to die,
Oh send a shining angel
　　To bear me to the sky.

4　Oh there I'll be an angel,
　　And with the angels stand,
A crown upon my forehead,
　　A harp within my hand;
And there before my Saviour,
　　So glorious and so bright,
I'll join the heavenly music,
　　And praise him day and night.

---

## 23.　I want to be like Jesus.

1. I WANT to be like Jesus,
　　So lowly and so meek,
For no one marked an angry word
　　That ever heard him speak.
I want to be like Jesus,
　　So frequently in prayer;
Alone upon the mountain-top
　　He met his Father there.

2. I want to be like Jesus;
　　I never, never find
That he, though persecuted, was
　　To any one unkind.

31

I want to be like Jesus,
  Engaged in doing good,
So that of me it may be said,
  "She hath done what she could."

3. I want to be like Jesus,
  So lowly and so meek
For no one marked an angry word
  That ever heard him speak.
Alas, I'm not like Jesus,
  As any one may see :
Oh, gentle Saviour, send thy grace
  And make me like to thee.

--------+--------

## 24.  The Precious Story.

1. How precious is the story
  Of our Redeemer's birth,
Who left the realms of glory,
  And came to dwell on earth :
He saw our sad condition,
  Our guilt and sin and shame ;
To save us from perdition
  The blessed Jesus came.

2. He came to earth from heaven,
  To weep and bleed and die,
That we might be forgiven,
  And raised to God on high.

His kindness and compassion
　To children then were shown;
The heirs of his salvation,
　He claimed them for his own.

3. Oh may I love this Saviour,
　So good, so kind, so mild ·
And may I find his favor,
　A young though sinful child
And in his blessed heaven
　May I at last appear,
With all my sins forgiven,
　To know and praise him there

---

## 25. Singing of Jesus.

1. Come, let us sing of Jesus,
　While hearts and accents blend,
Come, let us sing of Jesus,
　The sinner's only friend;
His holy soul rejoices
　Amid the choirs above,
To hear our youthful voices
　Exulting in his love.

2. We love to sing of Jesus,
　Who wept our path along;
We love to sing of Jesus,
　The tempted and the strong;

None who besought his healing,
   He passed unheeded by ;
And still retains his feeling
   For us above the sky.

3. We love to sing of Jesus,
   Who died our souls to save ;
We love to sing of Jesus,
   Triumphant o'er the grave ;
And in our hour of danger
   We 'll trust his love alone,
Who once slept in a manger,
   And now sits on the throne.

4. Then let us sing of Jesus,
   While yet on earth we stay,
And hope to sing of Jesus
   Throughout eternal day ;
For those who here confess him
   He will in heaven confess,
And faithful hearts that bless him
   He will for ever bless.

---

## 26.  To the Saviour Crucified.

1. O SACRED Head, now wounded,
   With grief and shame weighed down ,
Now scornfully surrounded
   With thorns, thy only crown ;

34

O sacred Head, what glory,
　What bliss till now was thine!
Yet, though despised and gory,
　I joy to call thee mine.

2. Oh noblest brow and dearest,
　In other days the world
All feared when thou appearedst.
　What shame on thee is hurled!
How art thou pale with anguish,
　With sore abuse and scorn;
How does that visage languish
　Which once was bright as morn!

3. What language shall I borrow
　To thank thee, dearest Friend,
For this thy dying sorrow,
　Thy pity without end?
Oh make me thine for ever;
　And should I fainting be,
Lord, let me never, never
　Outlive my love to thee.

4. Be near when I am dying;
　Oh show thy cross to me,
And for my succor flying.
　Come, Lord, to set me free.

These eyes new faith receiving,
From Jesus shall not move ;
For he who dies believing,
Dies safely, through thy love.

---

## 27. The Child's Desire.

1. I THINK, when I read
That sweet story of old,
When Jesus was here among men,
How he called little children
As lambs to his fold,
I should like to have been with them then.

2. I wish that his hands
Had been placed on my head,
That his arm had been thrown around me,
And that I might have seen
His kind look when he said,
"Let the little ones come unto me."

3. Yet still to his footstool
In prayer I may go,
And ask for a share in his love ;
And if I thus earnestly
Seek him below,
I shall see him and hear him above—

4. In that beautiful place
He has gone to prepare
For all who are washed and forgiven ;
 And many dear children
Are gathering there,
" For of such is the kingdom of heaven.'

---

## 28. Filial Affection.

1. BE kind to thy father,
For when thou wast young,
Who loved thee so fondly as he?
 He caught the first accents
That fell from thy tongue,
And joined in thy innocent glee.

2. Be kind to thy mother,
For lo, on her brow
May traces of sorrow be seen ;
 Oh well may'st thou cherish
And comfort her now,
For loving and kind she hath been.

3. Remember thy mother ;
For thee will she pray
As long as God giveth her breath
 With accents of kindness
Then cheer her lone way,
E'en to the dark valley of death.

## 29. Forbid Them Not.

1. WHEN many to the Saviour's feet
Their little children brought,
And from the source of blessedness
A Saviour's blessing sought;
To some who with mistaken zeal
The near approach forbade,
"Let little children come to me,"
The blessed Saviour said.

2. "Forbid them not, nor harshly chide
Their wish to see my face,
For little children such as these
My Father's kingdom grace."
Then gathered in his loving arms
And folded to his breast,
He poured a blessing all divine
On every little guest.

3. Dear children, Jesus is the same,
Though now enthroned above;
He waits to bless you as of old
With his forgiving love.
He marks with joy each faint attempt
His favor to obtain,
And those who early seek his face
Shall never seek in vain.

4. But sin prevents, and Satan strives
  To keep you from his arms ;
And to allure the soul away,
  The world displays its charms ;
But look to Jesus, for his power
  Your foes can ne'er withstand ;
Let him but say, "Forbid them not."
  They'll fly at his command.    A. A. G.

---

### 30. Come to the Saviour To-day.

1. Oh come to the Saviour,
Dear children, to-day,
'T s folly to wait till you 're older,
  The heart is now tender,
  But if you delay,
'T will surely grow harder and bolder.

CHORUS.

The Saviour is calling to-day ;
  He waits to receive you and save ;
Give heed to the warning,
Ere life's sunny morning
  Be closed in the night of the grave.

2. You hear of the cross
Where Immanuel bled,
And tears down your faces are stealing ;

But when a few years
Have rolled over your head,
You 'll hear of that cross without feeling.

CHORUS.

The Saviour is calling to-day;
He waits to receive you and save;
Give heed to the warning,
Ere life's sunny morning
Be closed in the night of the grave.

3. How many short graves
In the graveyard you see,
How many dear children there slumber;
And few may the days
Of your pilgrimage be;
No mortal can tell us their number.

4. Then fly to the Saviour,
Dear children, to-day,
While life's feeble taper is burning;
The Spirit now strives;
Should you grieve him away,
In vain may you wait his returning. A A G

---

### 31. While You 're Young.

1. OH wo n't you be a Christian
While you 're young?
Oh wo n't you be a Christian
While you 're young?

Do n't think it will be better
To delay it until later,
But remember your Creator
  While you 're young.

2. ‖:Oh wo n't you love the Saviour
  While you 're young?:‖
For you he left his glory
And embraced a cross so gory ;
Wo n't you heed the melting story
  While you 're young?

3. ‖:Remember, death may find you
  While you 're young : :‖
For friends are often weeping,
And the stars their watch are keeping
O'er the grassy graves, where sleeping
  Lie the young.

4. ‖:Oh walk the path to glory
  While you 're young ;:‖
And Jesus will befriend you,
And from danger will defend you,
And a peace divine will send you
  While you 're young.

5 Then wo n't you be a Christian
  While you 're young?
Then wo n't you be a Christian
  While you 're young?

41

Why from the future borrow,
When, ere comes another morrow,
You may weep in endless sorrow
While you're young?    A. A. G

## 82. This World's a Wilderness.

1. THIS world's a wilderness,
And dangers cluster round ;
There's not a traveller
But treads enchanted ground.
Oftentimes the scenes of woe
The flowing tears invite,
And joys depart, and sunny hours
Go out in gloomy night.

CHORUS.

Haste, haste, haste,
Haste to the world above ;
No sin is there, no grief or care,
But all is joy and love.

2. But walk in wisdom's ways,
And you shall happy be :
Jesus a refuge is,
For ever safe and free.

42

Let the storms of sorrow come,
  He 'll bid the tempest cease,
For wisdom's ways are pleasantness,
  And all her paths are peace.
    CHORUS—Haste, haste, haste, etc.

3. How bright the world appears
    When viewed by youthful eyes ;
  How sweet its cup of bliss,
    How fair its promises ;
  But 't is false as well as fair,
    The world is but a cheat,
  For every pleasure has a snare,
    A poison every sweet.

4. Turn, youthful traveller,
    Nor seek your portion here,
  Enter the path of life
    Where all is true and fair :
  Here are fruits that never cloy,
    And streams that never fail ;
  Oh feed thy soul with heavenly food
    While in this tearful vale.      ▲ ▲ G

## 33. Mercy's Call.

1. IN thy childhood's sunny morning,
    Ere the evil days draw nigh,
  Heed the Spirit's tender warning ;
    To the arms of Jesus fly.

Sin has lured thee and undone thee,
But in Jesus help is found ;
He will never, never shun thee,
For his mercy knows no bound.

2. Let not earthly joys delight thee,
Leave them all, and count them loss
Let not youthful follies fright thee,
Jesus bore them on the cross.
See the fountain ever flowing
For the guilty and defiled ;
Thousands to that fount are going,
Do thou likewise while a child.

3. There are pleasures never fading
In the pathway of the wise ;
And the weary pilgrim aiding
Jesus every want supplies :
He is ever near and precious,
Heals the wounded, cheers the faint ;
Taste and see how good and gracious
Jesus is to every saint.

4. Then in childhood's sunny morning.
Ere the heart is cold and hard,
From the downward pathway turning,
Mercy's tender call regard :
44

Ere the love of sin grows stronger,
   Ere the sober thoughts depart,
Ere the Spirit strives no longer,
   Youthful sinner, yield thy heart.

                  A. A G

---

## 34.  The Inquiry.

1. How can I be a happy child
   Where waves of trouble roll.
And drink of pleasures undefiled
   That satisfy the soul?
For all within and all around
   Is doomed to droop and die ;
Then where shall happiness be found,
   And who the want supply?

CHORUS.

'T is found in Jesus : yes, 't was he
   With blood the blessing bought :
'T was dear to him, 't is free to me ;
   It costs the sinner naught.

2. How can I be a holy child,
   And shun the downward road,
Where Satan reigns and sin has spoiled
   The noblest work of God?

How shall I tread enchanted ground,
  And keep my garments white;
And where shall conquering grace be found,
  And armor for the fight?
    CHORUS—'T is found in Jesus, etc.

3. How can I be a useful child,
  And feel for others' woes,
And make the desert drear and wild
  To blossom as the rose?
I 'll pray and toil and do my part,
  And ne'er to slumber yield;
But where 's the strength to keep my hea
  From fainting on the field?     *A.*

---

## 35. Just as I Am.

1. JUST as I am—without one plea,
  But that thy blood was shed for me,
  And that thou bidst me come to thee,
  O Lamb of God, I come, I come;
  Just as I am—without one plea,
  But that thy blood was shed for me.

2. Just as I am—and waiting not
  To rid my soul of one dark blot,
  To thee, who se blood can cleanse each spot,
  O Lamb of God, I come, I come!
    46

Just as I am—without one plea,
But that thy blood was shed for me.

3. Just as I am—though tossed about
With many a conflict, many a doubt,
Fightings within and fears without.
O Lamb of God, I come, I come!
     Just as I am, etc.

4. Just as I am—poor, wretched, blind;
Sight, riches, healing of the mind,
Yea, all I need, in thee to find,
O Lamb of God, I come, I come!

5. Just as I am—thou wilt receive,
Wilt welcome, pardon, cleanse, relieve;
Because thy promise I believe,
O Lamb of God, I come, I come!

6. Just as I am—thy love unknown
Has broken every barrier down;
Now to be thine, yea, thine alone,
O Lamb of God, I come, I come!
                              C. ELLIOTT.

## 36.  The Voice of Jesus.

1. I HEARD the voice of Jesus say,
     "Come unto me and rest;
Lay down, thou weary one, lay down
Thy head upon my breast."

• 47

I came to Jesus as I was,
   Weary and worn and sad ;
I found in him a resting-place,
   And he has made me glad.

2. I heard the voice of Jesus say,
   "Behold, I freely give
The living water ; thirsty one,
   Stoop down, and drink, and live."
I came to Jesus, and I drank
   Of that life-giving stream ;
My thirst was quenched, my soul revived,
   And now I live in him.

3. I heard the voice of Jesus say,
   "I am this dark world's light ;
Look unto me, thy morn shall rise,
   And all thy day be bright."
I looked to Jesus, and I found
   In him my star, my sun ;
And in that light of life I'll walk,
   Till travelling days are done.   BONAR.

## 37. The Heavenly Father.

1. Soon as I heard my Father say,
   "Ye children, seek my grace,"
My heart replied without delay,
   "I'll seek my Father's face."

Let not thy face be hid from me,
  Nor frown my soul away ;
God of my life, I fly to thee
  In each distressing day.

2. Should friends and kindred near and dear
  Leave me to want or die,
My God will make my life his care,
  And all my need supply.
Wait on the Lord, ye trembling saints,
  And keep your courage up ;
He 'll raise your spirit when it faints,
  And far exceed your hope.    WATTS.

---

## 3S.  Child of Grace.

1. How happy every child of grace,
  Who knows his sins forgiven !
This earth, he cries, is not my place,
  I seek my place in heaven :
A country far from mortal sight,
  Yet Oh, by faith I see
The land of rest, the saints' delight,
  The heaven prepared for me.

2. Oh what a blesséd hope is ours !
  While here on earth we stay,
We more than taste the heavenly powers,
  And antedate that day :

We feel the resurrection near—
Our life in Christ concealed—
And with his glorious presence here
Our earthen vessels filled.

3. Oh, would he more of heaven bestow!
And when the vessels break,
Let our triumphant spirits go
To grasp the God we seek;
In rapturous awe on him to gaze,
Who bought the sight for me,
And shout and wonder at his grace
To all eternity.          C. WESLEY.

### 39.   Christian Soldier.

1. AM I a soldier of the cross,
A follower of the Lamb,
And shall I fear to own his cause,
Or blush to speak his name
Shall I be carried to the skies
On flowery beds of ease,
While others fought to win the prize,
And sailed through bloody seas?

2. Are there no foes for me to face?
Must I not stem the flood?
Is this vain world a friend to grace,
To help me on to God?

Sure I must fight if I would reign ;
Increase my courage, Lord !
I 'll bear the toil, endure the pain,
Supported by thy word.

3. Thy saints, in all this glorious war,
Shall conquer, though they die ;
They see the triumph from afar ;
By faith they bring it nigh.
When that illustrious day shall rise,
And all thy armies shine
In robes of victory through the skies,
The glory shall be thine.        WATTS.

## 40.   Come to Jesus.

1. COME to Jesus, come to Jesus,
Come to Jesus to-day ;
To-day come to Jesus,
Come to Jesus to-day.

2. He will save you, he will save you,
He will save you to-day ;
To-day he will save you,
He will save you to-day.

3. Do n't reject him, do n't reject him,
Do n't reject him to-day,
To-day do n't reject him,
Do n't reject him to-day.

51

4. He is ready, he is ready,
   He is ready to-day ;
To-day he is ready,
   He is ready to-day.

5. Oh believe him, Oh believe him,
   Oh believe him to-day ;
To-day Oh believe him,
   Oh believe him to-day.

6. Do not tarry, do not tarry,
   Do not tarry to-day,
To-day do not tarry,
   Do not tarry to-day.

7. Hallelujah, hallelujah,
   Hallelujah, Amen,
Amen, hallelujah,
   Hallelujah, Amen.

The words *just now* can be used for *to-day*.

## 41. Faith in Christ.

1. My faith looks up to thee,
   Thou Lamb of Calvary,
      Saviour divine :
   Now hear me while I pray,
   Take all my guilt away ;
   Oh let me from this day
      Be wholly thine.

2. May thy rich grace impart
   Strength to my fainting heart,
      My zeal inspire :
   As thou hast died for me,
   Oh may my love to thee
   Pure, warm, and changeless be,
      A living fire.

3. While life's dark maze I tread,
   And griefs around me spread,
      Be thou my guide :
   Bid darkness turn to day,
   Wipe sorrow's tears away,
   Nor let me ever stray
      From thee aside.

4. When ends life's transient dream,
   When death's cold, sullen stream
      Shall o'er me roll,
   Blest Saviour, then in love
   Fear and distrust remove ;
   Oh bear me safe above,
      A ransomed soul.     PALMER.

---

## 42. God is Love.

1. COME, let us all unite to sing
        God is love!
   Let heaven and earth their praises bring,
        God is love.

Let every soul from sin awake,
Each in his heart sweet music make,
And sing with us, for Jesus' sake,
God is love.

2. Oh tell to earth's remotest bounds,
God is love!
In Christ we have redemption found ;
God is love.
His blood has washed our sins away,
His Spirit turned our night to day ;
And now we can rejoice to say
God is love.

3. How happy is our portion here !
God is love.
His promises our spirits cheer ;
God is love.
He is our sun and shield by day,
Our help, our hope, our strength, and stay ;
He will be with us all the way :
God is love.

4. What though my heart and flesh should fail !
God is love.
Through Christ I shall o'er death prevail :
God is love.

54

Though Jordan swell I need not fear,
My Saviour will be with me there,
My head above the waves to bear ;
   God is love!

5. In Zion we shall sing again,
   God is love.
Yes, this shall be our lofty strain,
   God is love.
While endless ages roll along,
In concert with the heavenly throng,
This shall be still our sweetest song,
   God is love!

---

## 43. Happy Day.

1. PRESERVED by thine almighty power,
 O Lord, our Maker, Saviour, King,
And brought to see this happy hour,
 We come thy praises here to sing.

### CHORUS.

Happy day, happy day,
Here in thy courts we 'll gladly stay,
And at thy footstool humbly pray
That thou wouldst take our sins away :
Happy day, happy day,
When Christ shall wash our sins away.

2. We praise thee for thy constant care,
   For life preserved, for mercies given ;
Oh may we still those mercies share,
   And taste the joys of sins forgiven.
      CHORUS—Happy day, happy day, etc.

3. And when on earth our days are done,
   Grant, Lord, that we at length may join,
Teachers and scholars round thy throne,
   The song of Moses and the Lamb.

## 44.   The Young Disciple.

1. OH happy day, that fixed my choice
   On thee, my Saviour and my God ;
Well may this glowing heart rejoice,
   And tell its raptures all abroad.

### CHORUS.

Happy day, happy day,
Here in thy courts we 'll gladly stay,
And at thy footstool humbly pray
That thou wouldst take our sins away :
Happy day, happy day,
When Christ shall wash our sins away.

2. 'T is done, the great transaction 's done,
   I am my Lord's, and he is mine :
He drew me, and I followed on,
   Charmed to confess the voice divine.
      CHORUS—Happy day, happy day, etc.

3. High heaven that heard the solemn vow,
   That vow renewed shall daily hear,
Till in life's latest hour I bow,
   And bless in death a bond so dear.

DODDRIDGE.

### 45. The Good Shepherd.

1. I WAS a wandering sheep,
   I did not love the fold;
I did not love my Shepherd's voice,
   I would not be controlled;
I was a wayward child,
   I did not love my home,
I did not love my Father's voice,
   I loved afar to roam.

2. The Shepherd sought his sheep,
   The Father sought his child;
They followed me o'er vale and hill,
   O'er deserts waste and wild:
They found me nigh to death,
   Famished and faint and lone;
They bound me with the bands of love,
   They saved the wandering one.

3. Jesus my Shepherd is;
   'T was he that loved my soul,
'T was he that washed me in his blood,
   'T was he that made me whole:

57

'T was he that sought the lost,
    That found the wandering sheep ;
'T was he that brought me to the fold ;
    'T is he that still doth keep.

4. No more a wandering sheep,
    I love to be controlled ;
I love my tender Shepherd's voice,
    I love the peaceful fold.
No more a wayward child,
    I seek no more to roam ;
I love my heavenly Father's voice ;
    I love, I love his home.    BONAR.

## 46. Jesus Ever Near.

1. DEAR Jesus, ever at my side,
    How loving must thou be,
To leave thy home in heaven to save
    A little child like me.

2. Thy beautiful and shining face
    I see not, though so near ;
The sweetness of thy soft low voice
    I am too deaf too hear.

3. But I have felt thee in my thought,
    Fighting with sin for me ;
And when my heart loves God, I know
    The sweetness is from thee.

4. And when, dear Saviour, I kneel down,
    Morning and night, to prayer,
  Something there is within my heart
    Which tells me thou art there.

5. Yes, when I pray, thou prayest too ;
    Thy prayer is all for me ;
  But when I sleep, thou sleepest not,
    But watchest patiently.

### 47. The Shepherd's Care.

1. SEE, the kind Shepherd. Jesus. stands,
    And calls his sheep by name ;
  Gathers the feeble in his arms,
    And feeds each tender lamb.

2. He 'll lead us to the heavenly streams
    Where living waters flow ;
  And guide us to the fruitful fields
    Where trees of knowledge grow.

3. When, wandering from the fold, we leave
    The straight and narrow way,
  Our faithful Shepherd still is near,
    To guide us when we stray.

4. The feeblest lamb amid the flock
    Shall be the Shepherd's care ;
  While folded in our Saviour's arms,
    We 're safe from every snare.

## 48. Song of Children.

1. ONCE was heard the song of children
    By the Saviour when on earth,
Joyful in the sacred temple
    Shouts of youthful praise had birth,

CHORUS.

‖:And hosannas, and hosannas,
    Loud to David's Son broke forth. :‖

2. Palms of victory strown around him,
    Garments spread beneath his feet,
Prophet of the Lord they crowned him
    In fair Salem's crowded street,
        ‖:While hosannas, while hosannas
    From the lips of children greet. :‖

3. Blesséd Saviour, now triumphant,
    Glorified and throned on high!
Mortal lays from man or infant
    Vain to tell thy praise may try ;
        ‖:But hosannas, but hosannas
    Swell the chorus of the sky. :‖

4. God o'er all, in heaven reigning,
    We this day thy glory sing ;
Not with palms thy pathway strewing—
    We would loftier tribute bring—
        ‖:Glad hosannas, glad hosannas
    To our Prophet, Priest, and King. :‖

## 49. The Saviour's Word.

1. How firm a foundation,
      Ye saints of the Lord,
   Is laid for your faith  ·
      In his excellent word :
   What more can he say
      Than to you he hath said,
   Who unto the Saviour
      For refuge have fled.

2. Fear not, I am with thee ;
      Oh be not dismayed,
   For I am thy God,
      And will still give thee aid :
   I' ll strengthen thee, help thee,
      And cause thee to stand,
   Upheld by my righteous
      Omnipotent hand.

3. When through the deep waters
      I call thee to go,
   The rivers of sorrow
      Shall not overflow ;
   For I will be with thee
      Thy trials to bless,
   And sanctify to thee
      Thy deepest distress.

4. The soul that on Jesus
   Hath leaned for repose,
I will not, I will not
   Desert to his foes :
That soul, though all hell
   Should endeavor to shake,
I 'll never—no, never—
   No, never forsake.      KIRKHAM.

---

## 50.  Christ our Friend.

1. How loving is Jesus
   Who came from the sky,
In tenderest pity
   For sinners to die :
His hands and his feet
   Were nailed to the tree,
And all this he suffered
   For you and for me.

2. How precious is Jesus
   To all who believe,
And out of his fulness
   What grace they receive :
When weak he supports them,
   When erring he guides,
And every thing needful
   He kindly provides.

3. Oh give then to Jesus
   Your earliest days ;
   They only are blessed
   .Who walk in his ways :
   In life and in death
   He will still be your Friend,
   For whom Jesus loveth,
   He loves to the end.

--------

## 51. The Rose of Sharon.

1. THERE is a Rose whose beauties grace
   The garden where it grows ;
   In lowly hearts it finds a place,
   'T is Sharon's lovely Rose.

   CHORUS.
   Beautiful Rose, beautiful Rose,
   ||:Rose of Sharon, beautiful Rose. :||

2. Unchanged by time, it never dies,
   Its beauties ne'er depart ;
   And not a thorn this Rose supplies,
   To pierce its home, the heart.
   CHORUS—Beautiful Rose, etc.

3. Though in this wilderness forlorn
   This lovely Rose is found,
   Before the morning stars were born
   It bloomed on heavenly ground.

4. Its fragrance filled the heavenly plains,
  And all the sons of earth
May prove the virtues it contains,
  And sing its wondrous worth.

5. In regions parched by burning heat,
  Or chilled by polar snows,
The Rose of Sharon we may meet,
  For Jesus is that Rose.   A. A. G

## 52. The Good Ship Zion.

1. We are homeward bound
  To the land of light and love
With a swelling sail we onward sweep;
  Though the rude winds blow,
  There is One who rules above,
Who will guard the weary sailor on the deep.

CHORUS.
In the good ship Zion
  We are tossing on the tide,
But the wild dark tempest soon shall cease
  All the danger over,
  She will safe at anchor ride
In the port of everlasting peace.

2. Though the billows rise,
  They shall never overwhelm.
Though the breakers roar upon the lee;
  64

'Mid the strife we'll sing,
For we've Jesus at the helm,
And he'll steer the good ship Zion o'er the sea.
Chorus—In the good ship Zion, etc.

3. Though for ages past
    She has ploughed the stormy main,
She's the stout ship Zion as of yore;
    Safe 'mid rocks and shoals
    And the fearful hurricane,
She has thousands brought to Canaan's happy
.    shore.

4. Ho, ye youthful souls,
    There is danger in your path,
By the chart of folly you're misled:
    There are rocks beneath,
    And above a storm of wrath,
And the breakers of destruction are ahead.

5. We are homeward bound;
    Won't you join our happy crew?
Come aboard, poor sinner, while you may:
    To the eye of faith
    There's the better land in view;
'Tis the land that shines with never-ending day.

A A G

## 53. The Land of Canaan.

1. COME, children, let us sweetly sing,
    We are bound for the land of Canaan;
All glory give to Christ our King,
    We are bound for the land of Canaan;
Oh, Canaan is our happy home,
    We are bound for the land of Canaan.
Oh, Canaan, bright Canaan,
    We are bound for the land of Canaan.

2. Happy are all good children here,
    They are bound for the land of Canaan;
And soon they'll be as angels are,
    They are bound for the land of Canaan;
Oh, Canaan is our happy home, etc.

3. Come then and join our happy band,
    We are bound for the land of Canaan;
To ever dwell at Christ's right hand,
    We are bound for the land of Canaan;
Oh, Canaan is our happy home, etc.

4. Then louder still our songs shall rise,
    We are bound for the land of Canaan—
When we are far beyond the skies;
    We are bound for the land of Canaan;
Oh, Canaan is our happy home, etc.

## 54. Glory, Glory, Glory!

1. HAPPY angels, still you dwell
   In yon worlds of glory,
And in joyous anthems swell
   Love's redeeming story.
Shining multitudes, ye came
   Our Redeemer to proclaim;
Still your song is just the same:
   Glory, glory, glory!

2. Angels, sing again with man,
   Swell our strain of glory;
Shout with us the wondrous plan,
   Love's redeeming story;
Soon our stay on earth shall fail,
Soon shall drop the mortal veil;
Then in strains like yours we'll hail,
   Glory, glory, glory!

3. Christ our Lord the theme, the song,
   Then no more the stranger
Welcomed by the shining throng
   In lone Bethlehem's manger:
Robed in peerless majesty,
Soon our eyes the Lord shall see;
Then we'll cry, "'T is he, 't is he!
   Glory, glory, glory!"

67

## 55. Millennial Dawn.

1. WATCHMAN, tell us of the night,
   What its signs of promise are.
   Traveller, o'er yon mountain's height
   See that glory-beaming star.
   Watchman, does its beauteous ray
   Aught of hope or joy foretell?
   Traveller, yes, it brings the day,
   Promised day of Israel.

2. Watchman, tell us of the night,
   Higher yet that star ascends;
   Traveller, blessedness and light,
   Peace and truth, its course portends.
   Watchman, will its beams alone
   Gild the spot that gave them birth?
   Traveller, ages are its own;
   See, it bursts o'er all the earth.

3. Watchman, tell us of the night,
   For the morning seems to dawn.
   Traveller, darkness takes its flight,
   Doubt and terror are withdrawn.
   Watchman, let thy wanderings cease;
   Hie thee to thy quiet home.
   Traveller, lo, the Prince of peace,
   Lo, the Son of God is come!          BOWRING.

## 56. Christ our Refuge.

1. JESUS, lover of my soul,
   Let me to thy bosom fly,
While the billows near me roll,
   While the tempest still is high;
Hide me, O my Saviour, hide,
   Till the storm of life is past;
Safe into the haven guide;
   Oh receive my soul at last.

2. Other refuge have I none;
   Hangs my helpless soul on thee;
Leave, ah, leave me not alone,
   Still support and comfort me:
All my trust on thee is stayed,
   All my help from thee I bring;
Cover my defenceless head
   With the shadow of thy wing.

3. Thou, O Christ, art all I want;
   More than all in thee I find:
Raise the fallen, cheer the faint,
   Heal the sick, and lead the blind.
Just and holy is thy name,
   I am all unrighteousness;
Vile and full of sin I am,
   Thou art full of truth and grace.

WESLEY.

## 57. Value of the Bible.

1. HOLY Bible, book divine,
Precious treasure, thou art mine!
Mine to tell me whence I came,
Mine to teach me what I am;
Mine to chide me when I rove,
Mine to show a Saviour's love;
Mine thou art to guide my feet;
Mine to judge, condemn, acquit;

2. Mine to comfort in distress,
If the Holy Spirit bless;
Mine to show, by living faith,
Man can triumph over death;
Mine to tell of joys to come,
And the rebel sinner's doom:
Oh thou precious book divine,
Precious treasure, thou art mine!

## 58. Pilgrim's Song.

1. CHILDREN of the heavenly King,
As ye journey, sweetly sing:
Sing your Saviour's worthy praise,
Glorious in his works and ways.
Ye are travelling home to God
In the way the fathers trod:
They are happy now, and ye
Soon their happiness shall see.

70

2. Shout, ye little flock and blest;
You on Jesus' throne shall rest:
There your seat is now prepared—
There your kingdom and reward.
Lord, submissive make us go,
Gladly leaving all below:
Only thou our leader be,
And we still will follow thee.  CENNICK

---

## 59.  Songs of Praise.

1. Songs of praise the angels sang,
Heaven with hallelujahs rang,
When Jehovah's work begun,
When he spake and it was done.
Songs of praise awoke the morn
When the Prince of peace was born;
Songs of praise arose when he
Captive led captivity.

2. Heaven and earth must pass away;
Songs of praise shall crown that day:
God will make new heavens and earth,
Songs of praise shall hail their birth.
And shall man alone be dumb
Till that glorious kingdom come?
No, the church delights to raise
Psalms and hymns and songs of praise.

71

3. Saints below, with heart and voice,
   Still in songs of praise rejoice ;
   Learning here, by faith and love,
   Songs of praise to sing above.
   Borne upon their latest breath,
   Songs of praise shall conquer death ;
   Then, amid eternal joy,
   Songs of praise their powers employ.

MONTGOMERY

## 60.  The Good Shepherd.

1. ONCE I wandered on the mountain,
      In the paths by sinners trod,
   Heeded not the flowing fountain,
      Trifled with atoning blood ;
   But the Shepherd kindly sought me,
      Guilty, wretched, and unclean,
   Pardoned all my sin, and brought me
      To his pastures fresh and green.

2. In this vale of tears and sadness,
      He 's my Shepherd, ever near,
   Turning all my grief to gladness,
      When on him I cast my care.
   Though a father may forsake me,
      And a mother sink to rest,
   Tender Shepherd, he will take me,
      Pierced by sorrow, to his breast.

3. Strong temptations may beset me,
   Snares my pathway may bestrew,
But he never will forget me.
   He will guard and guide me too.
He observes each poor endeavor
   To escape from sin's control,
And the sunshine of his favor
   Cheers my fainting, struggling soul.

4. When the shades of death o'erspread me,
   And the streams of life congeal,
Faithful Shepherd, do thou lead me
   Safely through the silent vale:
When I lay aside the mortal,
   Immortality to prove,
Bear me through the heavenly portal,
   Place me in thy fold above.　　ᴀ ᴀ ᴀ

---

## 61.  Sweetly Sing.

1. SWEETLY sing, sweetly sing
   Praises to our heavenly King;
   Let us raise, let us raise
   High our notes of praise;
   Praise to Him whose name is Love,
   Praise to Him who reigns above;
   Raise your songs, raise your songs,
   Now with thankful tongues.

2. Angels bright, angels bright,
   Robed in garments pure and white,
   Chant his praise, chant his praise,
   In melodious lays.
   But from that bright, happy throng
   Ne'er can come this sweetest song.
   "Redeeming love, redeeming love
   Brought us here above."

3. Far away, far away,
   We in sin's dark valley lay ;
   Jesus came, Jesus came,
   Blessed be his name !
   He redeemed us by his grace,
   Then prepared in heaven a place
   To receive, to receive
   All who will believe.

4. Now we know, now we know
   We from earth must shortly go ;
   Soon the call, soon the call
   Comes to one and all.
   Saviour, when *our* time shall come,
   Take us to our heavenly home ;
   There we 'll raise notes of praise,
   Through unending days.

MISS J. W. SAMPSON

## 62. Let us with a Joyful Mind.

1. LET us with a joyful mind
Praise the Lord, for he is kind,
For his mercies shall endure,
Ever faithful, ever sure.

2. Children, come, extol his might,
Join with saints and angels bright ;
For his mercies shall endure,
Ever faithful, ever sure.

3. All our wants he doth supply,
Loves to hear our humble cry ;
For his mercies shall endure,
Ever faithful, ever sure.

4. He of old our fathers blessed,
Led them to the land of rest ;
For his mercies shall endure,
Ever faithful, ever sure.

5. His own Son he sent to die,
Us to raise to joys on high ;
For his mercies shall endure,
Ever faithful, ever sure.

6. Let us then with gladsome mind,
Praise the Lord, for he is kind ;
For his mercies shall endure,
Ever faithful, ever sure.

## 63. Birth of the Saviour.

1. HARK, the herald angels sing,
   "Glory to the new-born King!
   Peace on earth and mercy mild,
   God and sinners reconciled."

2. Joyful, all ye nations rise,
   Join the triumph of the skies;
   With the angelic host proclaim,
   "Christ is born in Bethlehem."

3. Veiled in flesh the Godhead see,
   Hail the incarnate Deity;
   Pleased as man with men t' appear—
   Jesus our Emmanuel here.

4. Hail the heaven-born Prince of peace;
   Hail the Sun of righteousness!
   Light and life to all he brings,
   Risen with healing in his wings.

5. Mild he lays his glory by—
   Born, that man no more may die
   Born to raise the sons of earth;
   Born to give them second birth.

76

## 64. Jubilee of the World.

1 HARK the song of jubilee!
　　Loud as mighty thunders roar,
Or the fulness of the sea
　　When it breaks upon the shore :

2. Hallelujah! for the Lord
　　God omnipotent shall reign ;
Hallelujah! let the word
　　Echo round the earth and main.

3. See Jehovah's banner furled,
　　Sheathed his sword: he speaks:'tis done;
And the kingdoms of this world
　　Are the kingdoms of his Son.

4. He shall reign from pole to pole
　　With illimitable sway :
He shall reign, when, like a scroll,
　　Yonder heavens have passed away.

5. Then the end : beneath his rod
　　Man's last enemy shall fall ;
Hallelujah! Christ in God,
　　God in Christ, is all in all.

## 65. Of Such is the Kingdom.

1. ROUND the throne in glory
   Happy children throng,
And redemption's story
   Wakes the harp and song.
On the verdant mountain,
   By the shining stream,
Or the living fountain,
   Jesus is their theme.

CHORUS.

Glory to the Lamb,
   Praise him and adore;
Glory to the Lamb
   For evermore.

2. Robes of snowy whiteness,
   Beautiful and rare;
Crowns of radiant brightness,
   Such those children wear:
Safe from death's bereavement,
   Sorrow and the grave,
Free from sin's enslavement
   Victory's palm they wave.
      CHORUS—Glory to the Lamb, etc.

3. Now the skilful fingers
   Sweep the golden lyre;
Not a harper lingers
   In that ransomed choir;

Voices sweetly blending
　With the tuneful string,
To the throne ascending,
　Praise the heavenly King.

4. Children now sojourning
　In a world of sin,
From your follies turning,
　Strive to enter in :
Let your young affections
　Round the Saviour twine ;
And 'mid heaven's attractions
　You shall sing and shine.　　▲ ▲ ▲

---

## 66. Fount.

1. Come, thou Fount of every blessing,
　Tune my heart to sing thy grace ;
Streams of mercy never ceasing,
　Call for songs of loudest praise :
Teach me some melodious sonnet,
　Sung by flaming tongues above ;
Praise the mount—I'm fixed upon it—
　Mount of God's unchanging love.

2. Here I raise my Ebenezer ;
　Hither by thy help I'm come ;
And I hope, by thy good pleasure,
　Safely to arrive at home.

Jesus sought me when a stranger,
   Wandering from the fold of God;
He to rescue me from danger,
   Interposed his precious blood.

3. Oh to grace how great a debtor
   Daily I'm constrained to be!
Let that grace now, like a fetter,
   Bind my wandering soul to thee:
Prone to wander, Lord, I feel it—
   Prone to leave the God I love;
Here's my heart—Oh take and seal it,
   Seal it from thy courts above.
                  ROBINSON

## 67.  Friend Ever Near.

1. ONE there is above all others
   Well deserves the name of Friend;
His is love beyond a brother's,
   Costly, free, and knows no end.
Which of all our friends, to save us,
   Could or would have shed his blood?
But our Jesus died to have us
   Reconciled in him to God.

2. When he lived on earth abased,
   "Friend of sinners" was his name;
Now, above all glory raised,
   He rejoices in the same.

Oh for grace our hearts to soften!
Teach us, Lord, at length to love.
We, alas, forget too often
What a Friend we have above.

NEWTON.

---

### 68. Sinners Entreated.

1. SINNERS, will you scorn the message
Sent in mercy from above?
Every sentence, Oh how tender!
Every line is full of love :
Listen to it ;
Every line is full of love.

2. Hear the heralds of the gospel
News from Zion's King proclaim,
To each rebel sinner, "Pardon,
Free forgiveness in his name :"
How important!
Free forgiveness in his name!

3. Oh, ye angels hovering round us,
Waiting spirits, speed your way,
Hasten to the court of heaven,
Tidings bear without delay :
Rebel sinners
Glad the message will obey.  ALLEN.

## 69. Pilgrim's Guide.

1. Guide me, O thou great Jehovah,
   Pilgrim through this barren land ;
 I am weak, but thou art mighty,
   Hold me with thy powerful hand ;
     Bread of heaven,
   Feed me till I want no more.

2. Open, Lord, the crystal fountain
   Whence the healing streams do flow ;
 Let the fiery, cloudy pillar,
   Lead me all my journey through ;
     Strong Deliverer,
   Be thou still my strength and shield.

3. When I tread the verge of Jordan,
   Bid my anxious fears subside ;
 Death of death, and hell's destruction,
   Land me safe on Canaan's side :
     Songs of praises
   I will ever give to thee.          ROBINSON

## 70. Children's Voices.

1. Oh, childhood's happy voice, birdlike and
     sweet,
 What can so cheer us at home when we meet,
 Loving and worshipping at Jesus' feet.
   82

2. Children's hosannas were sweet to his ear,
   Who, now enthroned above, still bends to hear
   Songs and hosannas from little ones here.

3. Lo, where their Sabbath-school melodies ring,
   Listening and hovering on viewless wing,
   Angels beholding the face of their King.

4. Saviour, blest Saviour, prepare by thy love
   All the dear children to praise thee above,
   Warbling for ever in heaven's happy grove.

5. Let us on earth begin heaven's long employ,
   Soothing the sorrows our souls that annoy,
   Singing each day with an ever new joy.

------♦------

## 71. Love for Jesus.

1. Jesus, how can I but love thee,
      Jesus, so loving and mild!
   How can thy cross fail to move me?
      There didst thou die for a child.

### CHORUS.

Love of the heart, praise of the tongue.
Jesus my Saviour deserves from the young;
Jesus my Saviour deserves from the young.

2. There in the day of thy anguish,
Mocked by the guilty around,
There didst thou suffer and languish,
.Bleeding from many a wound.
    Chorus—Love of the heart, etc.

3. Where are the friends that clung to thee?
Thee they would never disown!
Now from a distance they view thee
Treading the wine-press alone.

4. Help me, my Saviour, to love thee,
Though thy dear name is reviled;
Then at thy bar I shall prove thee
Saviour and friend of thy child.

5. In that dear cross would I glory
Which the proud world may despise,
And let the wonderful story
Tune my sweet harp in the skies.

           A A G.

## 72. We Won't Give Up the Bible.

1. We won't give up the Bible,
God's holy book of truth,
The blessed staff of hoary age,
The guide of early youth,

84

The lamp which sheds a glorious light
  O'er every dreary road,
The voice which speaks a Saviour's love,
  And leads us home to God.

CHORUS.

We wo n't give up the Bible,
  God's holy book of truth,
The blessed staff of hoary age,
  ||: The guide of early youth. :||

2. We wo n't give up the Bible,
    For it alone can tell
  The way to save our ruined souls
    From perishing in hell.
  And it alone can tell us how
    We can have hopes of heaven,
  That through the Saviour's precious blood
    Our sins may be forgiven.
      CHORUS—We wo n't give up, etc.

3. We wo n't give up the Bible,
    We 'll shout it far and wide,
  Until the echo shall be heard
    Beyond the rolling tide ;
  Till all shall know that we, though young,
    Withstand each treacherous art,
  And that from God's own sacred word
    We 'll never, never part.

85

## 73. The Pearl that Worldlings Covet.

1. THE pearl that worldlings covet
    Is not the pearl for me ;
    Its beauty fades as quickly
      As sunshine on the sea.
But there's a pearl sought by the wise,
'T is called the pearl of greatest price,
    Though few its value see ;
    Oh. that's the pearl for me!
    Oh, that's the pearl for me!

2. The crown that decks the monarch
    Is not the crown for me ;
    It dazzles but a moment,
      Its brightness soon will flee.
But there's a crown prepared above
For all who walk in humble love ;
    For ever bright 't will be :
    ‖:Oh. that's the crown for me! :‖

3. The road that many travel
    Is not the road for me ;
    It leads to death and sorrow,
      In it I would not be.
But there's a road that leads to God.
'T is marked by Christ's most precious blood,
    The passage here is free :
    ‖:Oh, that's the road for me! :‖

4. The hope that sinners cherish
   Is not the hope for me ;
Most surely will they perish,
   Unless from sin made free :
... there 's a hope which rests in God,
And leads the soul to keep his word
   And sinful pleasures flee :
   ||:Oh, that 's the hope for me!:||

———•———

## 74. Have Courage to do Right.

1. If you would find salvation,
   And taste its joys below,
Do n't parley with temptation,
   But promptly answer, No!

CHORUS.

Have courage to do right,
Have courage to do right ;
The world may sneer, but never fear,
Have courage to do right.

2. If lured by sinful pleasure,
   Look upward and resist ;
For sorrow without measure
   Shall rend the guilty breast.
      CHORUS—Have courage, etc.

3. If sinners should revile you,
   With patience bear the cross;
Their aim is to defile you,
   And glory in your loss.

4. The world will strive to charm you,
   And Satan hurl the dart;
But who or what can harm you
   While Jesus guards the heart?

5. Stand up then for the truthful,
   Stand up then for the pure;
Let courage nerve the youthful
   The conflict to endure.    A. A. G

## 75. The Sunday-School Army.

1. OH. do not be discouraged,
   For Jesus is your friend;
Oh, do not be discouraged,
   For Jesus is your friend.
He will give you grace to conquer,
He will give you grace to conquer,
   And keep you to the end.

### CHORUS.

I'm glad I'm in this army,
||:Yes, I'm glad I'm in this army :||
And I'll battle for the school.
He will give you grace to conquer, etc.

88

2. Fight on, ye little soldiers,
    The battle you shall win ;
Fight on, ye little soldiers,
    The battle you shall win ;
For the Saviour is your Captain,
For the Saviour is your Captain,
    And he has vanquished sin.
        CHORUS—I 'm glad I 'm in, etc.

3. And when the conflict's over,
    Before him you shall stand ;
And when the conflict's over,
    Before him you shall stand ;
You shall sing his praise for ever,
You shall sing his praise for ever,
    In Canaan's happy land.

## 76. Always Speak the Truth.

1. BE the matter what it may,
    Always speak the truth ;
Whether work, or whether play,
    Always speak the truth.
Never from this rule depart,
Grave it deeply on your heart ;
Written 't is in Virtue's chart :
    Always speak the truth.

2. There's a charm in verity—
    Always speak the truth;
But there's meanness in a lie—
    Always speak the truth.
He is but a coward slave
Who, a present pain to waive,
Stoops to falsehood: then be brave,
    Always speak the truth.


3 Falsehood seldom stands alone—
    Always speak the truth;
One begets another one—
    Always speak the truth.
Falsehood all the soul degrades,
'T is a sin which often breeds
Greater sins and darker deeds;
    Always speak the truth.


4. When you're wrong the folly own;
    Always speak the truth;
Here's a victory to be won;
    Always speak the truth.
He who speaks with lying tongue
Adds to wrong a greater wrong;
Then with courage true and strong
    Always speak the truth.

A. A. G

## 77. Sing His Praise.

1. WOULD you be as angels are?
Sing, Oh sing his praise ;
Would you banish every care?
Sing, Oh sing his praise ;
Like the lark upon the wing,
Like the warbling bird of spring,
Like the crystal spheres that ring,
Sing, Oh sing his praise.

2. If the world upon you frown,
Sing, Oh sing his praise ;
If you 're left to sing alone,
Sing, Oh sing his praise ;
If sad trials come to you,
As to every one they do,
For that they are blessings too,
Sing, Oh sing his praise.

## 78. Expostulation.

1. OH turn ye, Oh turn ye, for why will ye die?
Since God in great mercy is coming so nigh,
Since Jesus invites you, the Spirit says, Come,
And angels are waiting to welcome you home.

2. How vain the delusion that, while you delay,
   Your hearts may grow better, your chains
       melt away :
   Come wretched, come guilty, come just as
       you are ;
   All helpless and dying, to Jesus repair.

3. The contrite in heart he will freely receive :
   Oh why will you not the glad message believe?
   If sin be your burden, Oh, will you not come!
   'Tis he makes you welcome ; he bids you
       come home.

### 79.  To-Day.

1. To-DAY the Saviour calls :
       Ye wanderers, come :
   Oh, ye benighted souls,
       Why longer roam ?

2. To-day the Saviour calls :
       For refuge fly ;
   The storm of vengeance falls,
       Ruin is nigh.

3. To-day the Saviour calls ;
       Oh listen now :
   Within these sacred walls
       To Jesus bow

4. The Spirit calls to-day ;
   Yield to his power ;
   Oh grieve him not away,
   'T is mercy's hour.

---

## 80. Cross and Crown.

1. MUST Jesus bear his cross alone,
   And all the world go free?
   No, there 's a cross for every one,
   And there 's a cross for me.

2. How happy are the saints above,
   Who once went sorrowing here ,
   But now they taste unmingled love,
   And joy without a tear.

3. The consecrated cross I 'll bear
   Till death shall set me free,
   And then go home my crown to wear,
   For there 's a crown for me.      ALLEN.

---

## 81. Grateful Love to Christ.

1 ALAS, and did my Saviour bleed,
   And did my Sovereign die?
   Would he devote that sacred head
   For such a worm as I?

2. Was it for crimes that I had done
　He groaned upon the tree?
　Amazing pity, grace unknown,
　And love beyond degree!

3. Well might the sun in darkness hide,
　And shut his glories in,
　When Christ the mighty Saviour died
　For man the rebel's sin.

4. Thus might I hide my blushing face
　While his dear cross appears,
　Dissolve my heart in thankfulness,
　And melt mine eyes in tears.

5. But drops of grief can ne'er repay
　The debt of love I owe;
　Here, Lord, I give myself away,
　'Tis all that I can do.　　　　WATTS

---

## 82.　Christ our Refuge.

1. THE Saviour! Oh what endless charms
　Dwell in the blissful sound!
　Its influence every fear disarms,
　And spreads sweet comfort round.

2. Oh the rich depths of love divine!
　Of bliss a boundless store!
　Dear Saviour, let me call thee mine;
　I cannot wish for more.

94

3. On thee alone my hope relies,
    Beneath thy cross I fall—
My Lord, my Life, my Sacrifice,
    My Saviour and my All.

## 83. Brotherly Love.

1. How sweet, how heavenly is the sight,
    When those who love the Lord
In one another's peace delight,
    And thus fulfil his word.

2. When each can feel his brother's sigh,
    And with him bear a part;
When sorrow flows from eye to eye,
    And joy from heart to heart.

3. When, free from envy, scorn, and pride,
    Our wishes all above,
Each can his brother's failings hide,
    And show a brother's love.

4. Let love, in one delightful stream,
    Through every bosom flow;
And union sweet and dear esteem
    In every action glow.

5. Love is the golden chain, that binds
    The happy souls above;
And he's an heir of heaven, who finds
    His bosom glow with love.          SWAIN

## 84. The Pasture.

1. FAITHFUL Shepherd, meek and mild,
To thy pastures lead a child,
Where the tender verdure grows,
Where the peaceful streamlet flows,
Where thy flock, from danger free,
Hear thy voice, and follow thee.

2. There, beneath thy watchful eye,
They are safe, though danger's nigh;
There, enfolded in thy arms,
They can smile at rude alarms;
Though a host their way oppose,
Thou wilt save them from their foes.

3. When the vale of grief they tread,
Thou dost mark the tears they shed.
By their side in pity stand,
Dry the tear with tender hand;
Gently quell the rising fear,
Make it sweet to suffer there.

4. Faithful Shepherd, meek and mild,
To thy pastures lead a child;
Weak and helpless, Lord, I am,
Gather in a wandering lamb;
Lest from thee I further stray,
Take me to thy fold, I pray.

## 85. Pilgrim's Song.

1. BLESSED are the sons of God;
They are bought with Jesus' blood,
They are ransomed from the grave;
Life eternal they shall have:
With them numbered may we be,
Here and in eternity.

2. They are justified by grace,
They enjoy the Saviour's peace:
All their sins are washed away;
They shall stand in God's great day:
With them numbered may we be,
Here and in eternity.

3. They are lights upon the earth,
Children of a heavenly birth;
One with God, with Jesus one;
Glory is in them begun:
With them numbered may we be,
Here and in eternity.               HUMPHRIES

---

## 86. The Conflict.

1. Oh why do I find it so hard to do right?
The good are the happy, I know;
And why should I ever in sin take delight,
When sin is the parent of woe?

I vanity love, and I folly pursue,
   I yield me to passion's control,
My wishes are faint and my struggles are few
   For that which can solace the soul.

2. I never did wrong but a something within
   Admonished and blamed me the while;
I never did right but that something again
   Approved and allured by its smile.
I 'm not in a region of heathenish night,
   Then why to the sinful belong?
I know it is better by far to do right,
   Then why do I follow the wrong?

3. I dwell in the midst of pollution and crime,
   And all is disorder within;
I 'm lured by the glittering baubles of time,
   A captive to Satan and sin.
Thus helpless and hopeless, dear Saviour, I cry
   For purity, pardon, and peace;
Oh let me no more in captivity lie,
   But grant me a happy release.    .

4. I question no longer thy power to redeem,
   My soul on thy merit depends;
I see in the cross, with its red flowing stream,
   The fountain to save and to cleanse:
   98

Renewed by thy grace, I will walk in the light
  While others to darkness belong ;
Oh then 't will be easy to follow the right,
  And easy to turn from the wrong. ▲ ▲ ⊙

---

### 87. There 's a Crown for the Young.

1. I KNOW there 's a crown
  For the saints of renown,
And for saints whose good deeds are unsung,
  But Oh say, is it true,
  If their days are but few,
That a crown is laid up for the young?

CHORUS.

  Yes, yes, yes,
I know there 's a crown for the young ;
  If their lives daily prove
  That the Saviour they love,
I know there 's a crown for the young.

2. The youthful shall stand
  In that beautiful land,
And the song of salvation shall sing ;
  And the infant of days
  Strike its harp in the praise
Of Immanuel, its Saviour and King.
  CHORUS—Yes, yes, yes, etc.

3. The noble of birth,
    And the poor of the earth,
Both the man and the youth and the child,
    If in Jesus they trust,
    When they rise from the dust
Shall be crowned in the land undefiled.

4. The soul of a child,
    Though by folly defiled,
Is more precious than tongue can express ;
    And redeemed by the blood
    That on Calvary flowed,
It shall shine in the region of bliss.

5. Then be it your care
    For that world to prepare ;
Bear the cross, that the crown may be yours:
    Never tire in the road
    That leads upward to God,
For the crown is for him who endures.

A. A. G.

## 88.  Youthful Mariners.

1. Down the stream of life they glide,
    Little mariners so frail ;
Gently heaves the swelling tide,
    Softly blows the favoring gale.

They suspect no danger nigh,
Cloudless is the summer sky ;
Joy lights up each youthful eye
   As they gayly sail.

2. But the angry storm may blow,
   And the smiling heavens grow dark ;
And the hidden rocks below
   Rudely tear the trembling bark ;
Oft upon the listening ear
Falls the shriek of wild despair,
From the shipwrecked mariner
   In his shattered bark.

3. Heavenly Pilot, be our guide,
   Youthful mariners defend ;
O'er the winds and waves preside,
   In the dangerous hour befriend ;
Thou who bad'st the tempest cease,
And from peril didst release,
Guide them to the port of peace,
   Where their fears shall end.   A A G

---

## 89. The Heavenly Stranger.

1. BEHOLD a Stranger at the door :
He gently knocks, has knocked before ;
Has waited long, is waiting still ;
You treat no other friend so ill.

2. Oh lovely attitude—he stands
   With melting heart and loaded hands!
   Oh matchless kindness! and he shows
   This matchless kindness to his foes.

3. But will he prove a Friend indeed?
   He will: the very Friend you need:
   The Friend of sinners; yes. 't is He,
   With garments dyed on Calvary.

4. Rise, touched with gratitude divine,
   Turn out his enemy and thine,
   That soul-destroying monster sin,
   And let the heavenly Stranger in.

5. Admit him, ere his anger burn—
   His feet, departed, ne'er return:
   Admit him, or the hour's at hand
   You'll at his door rejected stand.   GREEN

---

### 90. Sinners Entreated.

1. "Come hither, all ye weary souls,
      Ye heavy-laden sinners, come:
   I'll give you rest from all your toils,
      And raise you to my heavenly home.

2. "They shall find rest that learn of me:
      I'm of a meek and lowly mind;
   But passion rages like the sea,
      And pride is restless as the wind.

3. "Blest is the man whose shoulders take
   My yoke, and bear it with delight:
My yoke is easy to his neck,
   My grace shall make the burden light."

WATTS

## 91. Joy over the Convert.

1. WHO can describe the joys that rise
   Through all the courts of Paradise,
To see a prodigal return,
To see an heir of glory born?

2. With joy the Father doth approve
   The fruit of his eternal love;
The Son with joy looks down and sees
The purchase of his agonies;

3. The Spirit takes delight to view
   The holy, soul he formed anew;
And saints and angels join to sing
The growing empire of their King.

WATTS

## 92. The Star of Bethlehem.

. WHEN, marshalled on the nightly plain,
   The glittering host bestud the sky,
One star alone of all the train
   Can fix the sinner's wandering eye.

2. Hark, hark! to God the chorus breaks,
   From every host, from every gem ;
But one alone the Saviour speaks,
   It is the Star of Bethlehem.

3. Once on the raging seas I rode—
   The storm was loud, the night was dark,
The ocean yawned—and rudely blowed
   The wind that tossed my foundering bark.

4. Deep horror then my vitals froze ;
   Death-struck, I ceased the tide to stem ;
When suddenly a star arose—
   It was the Star of Bethlehem.

5. It was my guide, my light, my all,
   It bade my dark forebodings cease ;
And through the storm and danger's thrall,
   It led me to the port of peace.

6. Now, safely moored, my perils o'er,
   I'll sing, first in night's diadem,
For ever and for evermore,
   The Star—the Star of Bethlehem!

H. K. WHITE.

## 93.   Christ our Refuge.

1. WHEN I survey the wondrous cross
   On which the Prince of glory died,
My richest gain I count but loss,
   And pour contempt on all my pride.

104

, 2. Forbid it, Lord, that I should boast,
　　Save in the death of Christ my God ;
　All the vain things that charm me most
　　I sacrifice them to his blood.

3. See, from his head, his hands, his feet,
　　Sorrow and love flow mingled down!
　Did e'er such love and sorrow meet,
　　Or thorns compose so rich a crown?

4. Were the whole realm of nature mine,
　　That were a present far too small ;
　Love so amazing, so divine,
　　Demands my soul, my life, my all.

WATTS

----

PRAISE God, from whom all blessings flow ;
Praise him, all creatures here below ;
Praise him above, ye heavenly host ;
Praise Father, Son, and Holy Ghost.

----

## 94. Sing Praises.

1. IN the rosy light
　Of the morning bright,
Lift the voice of praise on high,
　From the lips of youth
　To the God of truth,
Let the joyful echoes fly.

CHORUS.

Sing praises, glad praises,
 Sing, children, sing;
Let your songs arise
To the lofty skies,
 And exult in God our King.

2. As he looked in love
 From the world above,
Our distresses filled his eye;
 And a world to save,
 His Son he gave
On the bloody tree to die.
 CHORUS—Sing praises, etc.

3. Let his praise be spread;
 For the Lamb who bled
To deliver us from woe
 Has endured the cross,
 The disgrace, the loss;
Let his praise for ever flow.

4. Now exalted high
 O'er the earth and sky,
He delights in mercy still;
 Bends his gracious ear
 Our requests to hear,
And our longing souls to fill.

106

5. On the cross he hung
   For the old and young,
But he loves the children best ;
   To his arms we'll fly,
   On his grace rely,
And secure his promised rest.

---·---

## 95. Gentle Shepherd.

1. FAR from the fold of Jesus,
   I, a wayward child,
Like a straying lamb had wandered
   Into deserts wild ;
But the gentle Shepherd sought me,
   Won me by his charms ;
Safe away from danger brought me.
   In his loving arms.

### CHORUS.

Praise Jesus, gentle Shepherd,
   Saviour, loving, mild ;
Jesus' name is sweetest music
   To the Christian child.

2. To his bosom close he pressed me,
   Pardoned all my sin,
Led me by the stillest waters
   Into pastures green.

Now all day I'm glad and joyful,
　　Happy in his love;
All the night my rest is peaceful,
　　Guarded from above.
　　　　CHORUS—Praise Jesus, etc.


3. Evermore I'll trust in Jesus,
　　He shall be my guide;
No allurement shall entice me
　　From my Shepherd's side.
By-and-by, from earth's temptations
　　He will give me rest,
And in heaven's greener pastures
　　Make me ever blest.

————·————

## 96.　The Name of Jesus.

1. How sweet the name of Jesus sounds
　　In a believer's ear;
It soothes his sorrows, heals his wound
And drives away his fear.

### CHORUS.

I do believe, I now believe
　　That Jesus died for me;
And through his blood, his precious bloc
　　I shall from sin be free.
108

2. It makes the wounded spirit whole,
    And calms the troubled breast ;
'T is manna to the hungry soul,
    And to the weary rest.
        CHORUS—I do believe, etc.

3. By him my prayers acceptance gain,
    Although with sin defiled ;
Satan accuses me in vain,
    And I am owned a child.

4. Weak is the effort of my heart,
    And cold my warmest thought ;
But when I see thee as thou art,
    I 'll praise thee as I ought.

5. Till then I would thy love proclaim
    With every fleeting breath ;
And may the music of thy name
    Refresh my soul in death.        NEWTON.

## 97.  The Sunday-school.

1. THE Sunday-school, that blessed place,
    Oh, I would rather stay
Within its walls, a child of grace,
    Than spend my hours in play,

CHORUS.

The Sunday-school, the Sunday-schoo
  Oh, 't is the place I love ;
For there I learn the golden rule,
  And sing of joys above.

2. 'T is there I learn that Jesus died
  For sinners such as I ;
Oh what has all this world beside
  That I should prize so high ?
      CHORUS—The Sunday-school, etc.

3. Then let our grateful tribute rise,
  And songs of praise be given
To Him who dwells above the skies,
  For such a blessing given.

4. And welcome then the Sunday-school
  We 'll read and sing and pray,
And learn by heart the golden rule,
  And never from it stray.

---

## 98.  Faith.

1. FAITH is a very simple thing,
  Though little understood ;
It frees the soul from death's dread sti
  By resting in Christ's blood.

110

CHORUS.

I do believe, I now believe,
  That Jesus died for me ;
And through his blood, his precious blood,
  I shall from sin be free.

2. It sees, upon the throne of God,
   A victim that was slain ;
   It rests its all on his shed blood,
   And says, "I'm born again."
     CHORUS—I do believe, etc.

3. What Jesus is, and that alone,
   Is faith's delightful plea ;
   It neither rests on *sinful* self,
   Nor *righteous* self, in me.

4. The perfect One that died for me,
   Draws near his Father's throne,
   Presents our names before our God,
   And pleads himself alone.

## 99.  Home of the Blest.

1. Oh happy land, Oh happy land,
   Where saints and angels dwell ;
   We long to join that glorious band,
   And all their anthems swell.

111

CHORUS.

Oh heaven dear, the happy home
Of all the pure and blest ;
I long to share thy mansions fair,
And be with Christ at rest.

2. But every voice in yonder throng
On earth has breathed a prayer ;
No lips untaught may join that song,
Or learn the music there.
CHORUS—Oh heaven dear, etc.

3. Thou heav'nly Friend, thou heav'nly Friend.
Oh hear us when we pray :
Now let thy pardoning grace descend,
And take our sins away.

4. Be all our fresh, our youthful days
To thy blest service given ;
Then we shall meet to sing thy praise,
A ransomed band in heaven.

## 100. The Fountain for Sinners.

1. THERE is a fountain filled with blood
Drawn from Immanuel's veins ;
And sinners plunged beneath that flood
Lose all their guilty stains.

112

CHORUS.

Our sorrows and our sins were laid
  On thee, alone on thee ;
Thy precious blood our ransom paid ;
  Thine all the glory be.

2. The dying thief rejoiced to see
  That fountain in his day ;
And there may I, as vile as he,
  Wash all my sins away.
    CHORUS—Our sorrows, etc.

3. Dear dying Lamb, thy precious blood
  Shall never lose its power
Till all the ransomed church of God
  Be saved, to sin no more.
    CHORUS—Our sorrows, etc.

4. E'er since, by faith, I saw the stream
  Thy flowing wounds supply,
Redeeming love has been my theme,
  And shall be till I die.

5. Then in a nobler, sweeter song,
  I 'll sing thy power to save ;
When this poor lisping, stam'ring tongue
  Lies silent in the grave.    COWPER.

## 101. Full Salvation.

1. For ever here my rest shall be,
Close to thy bleeding side ;
This all my hope and all my plea—
For me the Saviour died.

CHORUS.

I do believe, I now believe,
That Jesus died for me ;
And through his blood, his precious blood,
I shall from sin be free.

2. My dying Saviour and my God,
Fountain for guilt and sin,
Sprinkle me ever with thy blood,
And cleanse and keep me clean.
Chorus—I do believe, etc.

3. Wash me, and make me thus thine own,
Wash me, and mine thou art ;
Wash me, but not my feet alone—
My hands, my head, my heart.

4. The atonement of thy blood apply,
Till faith to sight improve ;
Till hope in full fruition die,
And all my soul be love.

118

### Chorus.

Our sorrows and our sins were laid
  On thee, alone on thee;
Thy precious blood our ransom paid;
  Thine all the glory be.

———•———

## 102. Invitation.

1. Come to the Sabbath-school,
   We really wish you would;
   Wo n't you come and join a class?
   We'll surely do you good.
   Bright eyes and happy hearts,
   And voices sweet and clear.
   Just walk in and look around,
   You'll surely find them here.

#### CHORUS.

Come then, for now's the time;
Come in your youthful prime,
Come when you 're free from crime;
Come, come, come.

2. Hark, 't is the signal bell;
   So wo n't you come along?
   Gladly will we welcome you,
   And greet you with a song.

Do n't say your clothes are poor;
I 'm sure they might be worse,
Be you rich, or be you poor,
It matters not to us.
CHORUS—Come then, etc.

3. List to the voice within ;
It gently whispers, "Go :"
That which makes you hesitate
Most surely is your foe ;
Make now the wise resolve,
And firmly say, "I will;"
Then you 'll overcome the foe,
And peace your heart shall fill.

4. Come then to Sabbath-school ;
There 's nothing there to fear ;
There are pleasant works to do,
And pleasant words to hear :
There do we learn the way
How sin may be forgiven ;
There we train for usefulness,
And there we train for heaven. A. A. G

## 103.  Sabbath Morning.

1. OH the Sabbath morning, beautiful and bright,
Joyfully we hail its golden light,
All the gloomy shadows chasing far away,
Bringing us the pleasant day.

Day calm and holy, day nearest heaven,
Day which a Father's love has given;
Oh the Sabbath morning, beautiful and bright,
Glad we hail its golden light.

2. All the days of labor ended one by one,
Glad are we the six days' work is done;
Glad to have a day of sweet and holy rest;
'T is the day that God has blest.
Chorus—Day calm and holy, etc.

3. Let us spend the moments of this holy day,
So that when they all have passed away,
Sweet 't will be to think, the quiet Sabbath
even
Brings us one day nearer heaven.
Chorus—Day calm and holy, etc.
MISS J. W. SAMPSON.

## 104. Remember the Sabbath-School.

. 1. Oh, remember the Sabbath-school
When the summer is past,
And the chill winds sigh mournfully,
And the snow-flakes fly fast.

Do not say, "It looks drearily;
'T is a cold wintry day;"
Come with eyes sparkling merrily;
Come, boys and girls, away.

CHORUS.

Yes, away to the Sabbath-school,
The Sabbath-school, the Sabbath-school;
Yes, away to the Sabbath-school,
The blessed Sabbath-school.

2. When the spring buds are opening,
    To the school you repair;
When the summer flower's blossoming,
    Oh you love to be there:
Like the bright and the beautiful,
    Love to honor God's day;
Come with hearts warm and dutiful,
    Come, boys and girls, away.
        CHORUS—Yes, away to the, etc.

3. Oh the same friends will meet you there,
    And around you will cling;
And the same songs will greet you there
    That you sung in the spring:
And the same truths address you there,
    And if you will obey,
The dear Saviour will bless you there,
    Then, boys and girls, away.          A. L. W.
118

## 105. Jesus Loves Me.

1. JESUS loves me, this I know,
   For the Bible tells me so.
   Little ones to him belong ;
   They are weak, but he is strong.

2. Jesus loves me, he who died
   Heaven's gate to open wide ;
   He will wash away my sin,
   Let his little child come in.

3. Jesus loves me, loves me still,
   Though I 'm very weak and ill ;
   From his shining throne on high
   Comes to watch me where I lie.

4. Jesus loves me ; he will stay
   Close beside me all the way :
   If I love him, when I die
   He will take me home on high.

---

## 106. The Good Shepherd.

1. IN the Saviour's pleasant fold,
   Sheltered from the heat and cold,
   Guarded from the dangers round,
   We thy little lambs are found.

2. None can ever hurt us there,
Safe within our Shepherd's care;
For, if any foe alarms,
He will clasp us in his arms.

3. Saviour, by thy tender grace,
Grant us in thy fold a place;
May we listen to thy voice,
And to do thy will rejoice.

4. Day by day, while here below,
May we wiser, happier grow;
Thus preparing in thy love
For the better fold above.    NEW LUTE.

## 107.  Come into Christ's Army.

1. COME into Christ's army,
Come, join it to-day;
He calls us himself,
So we must not delay.
What though we are children,
We're never too small
To be soldiers for Jesus;
So come one and all.

CHORUS.

||:Christ gives us our watchword;
'T is written above
On the folds of our banner—
That watchword is LOVE. :||

2. He gives us our armor,
    So shining and bright,
So let us fight bravely
    For truth and for right;
The foes we must conquer
    Are strong ones indeed:
We must ask for His help,
    Or we shall not succeed.
        CHORUS—Christ gives us, etc.


3. We've plenty of trials
    And dangers to meet,
And Satan our foe
    Oft will threaten defeat;
Temptation too often
    Will lead us astray;
But our Captain stands ready
    To show us our way.
        CHORUS—Christ gives us, etc.


4. He'll keep us in safety
    Till life shall be o'er;
E'en Death cannot harm us—.
    Christ met him before;
We'll follow our Leader
    Till yonder bright heaven
Shall ring with our praises
    For victory given.

## 108. Will You Meet us.

1. SAY, brothers, will you meet us,
   Say, brothers, will you meet us,
   Say, brothers, will you meet us,
   On Canaan's happy shore?

2. By the grace of God we'll meet you,
   By the grace of God we'll meet you,
   By the grace of God we'll meet you,
   Where parting is no more.

3. Jesus lives and reigns for ever,
   Jesus lives and reigns for ever,
   Jesus lives and reigns for ever,
   On Canaan's happy shore.

4. Glory, glory, hallelujah,
   Glory, glory, hallelujah,
   Glory, glory, hallelujah,
   For ever, evermore.

## 109. Let us Work for the School.

1. LET us work for the school
   With our hearts and our hands ;
   Let it never, no, never decline ;
   For its praises are sung
   By the good in all lands
   That are blest with the gospel divine.

Rally then, rally then,
Stand by the school ;
Why should it languish and die?
Rally then, rally then,
Stand by the school ;
Why should it languish and die?

2. 'T is perfumed by the prayers,
    'T is bedewed by the tears
Of the holy, the active, the true ;
They rejoiced at its hopes,
    And they mourned at its fears,
When its friends were but feeble and few.
        CHORUS—Rally then, rally then, etc.

3. Now the sunshine of favor
    Illumines its path,
And the church spreads above it her wing;
'T is a source of her weal,
    'T is a source of her worth,
And a gem in the crown of her King.

4. There are thousands now singing
    And shining above,
There are thousands now toiling below,
Who were melted and won
    By Immanuel's love,
As they heard in the school of his woe.

## 110. Over the Sea.

1. THE sea is wildly tossing,
   And often clothed with gloom,
   On which we 're swiftly crossing
   To our eternal home.

   CHORUS.

   Over the sea, over the sea,
   Gracious Saviour, pilot me ;
   Over the sea, over the sea,
   Spirit kind, my guardian be ;
   Over the sea, wherever I roam,
   Father above, Oh bring me home
   Under the bright celestial dome.

2. We 've many a foe to conquer,
   And many a storm to face,
   Ere we in heaven may anchor,
   And sing redeeming grace.
   CHORUS—Over the sea, etc.

3. Though nature in commotion
   Defy our power and skill,
   Our Jesus rules the ocean,
   And bids the winds be still.

4. Sail on then, comrades, boldly,
   And make God's word your chart ;
   Do every duty nobly,
   With joyful, trustful heart.

5. We'll float the gospel banner,
   And guard it with our life,
And shout at last, "Hosanna,"
   Victorious in the strife.

## 111. Morning Hymn.

1. THE morning, the bright
   And the beautiful morning
Is up, and the sunshine
   Is all on the wing,
With its fresh flush of gladness
   The landscape adorning—
A gladness which nothing
   But morning can bring.
The earth is awaking,
   The sky and the ocean,
The river and forest,
   The mountain and plain,
The city is stirring
   Its living commotion,
And the pulse of the world
   Is reviving again.

2. And we too awake
   For our heavenly Father,
Who soothed us so gently
   To sleep on his breast,

And made the soft stillness
Of evening to gather
Around us, now calls us
Again from our rest.
But ere to our studies
And duties returning,
We hasten to give him
The praise that is meet,
And in solemn devotion,
The first hours of morning,
Our freest and freshest,
We lay at his feet.

3. Then away to the school
In the sweet summer morning,
God's blessing upon us,
His light on our road ;
And let all the lessons
We're happily learning,
Be only to bring us
More surely to God.
Oh, now let us haste
To our heavenly Father,
And ere the fair skies
Of life's dawning be dim,
Let us come with glad hearts,
Let us come all together,
And the morn of our youth
Let us hallow to him.         BONAR.

## 112. The Eden Above.

1. How sweet to reflect
   On the joys that await me
In yon blissful region,
   The haven of rest,
Where glorified spirits
   With welcome shall greet me,
And lead me to mansions
   Prepared for the blest;
Encircled with light,
   And with glory enshrouded,
My happiness perfect,
   My mind's sky unclouded,
I'll bathe in the ocean
   Of pleasure unbounded,
And range with delight
   Through the Eden above.

2. Then hail, blessed state;
   Hail, ye songsters of glory,
Ye harpers of bliss,
   Soon I'll meet you above,
And join your full choir
   In rehearsing the story,
"Salvation from sorrow
   Through Jesus' dear love."

Then songs to the Lamb
  Shall reëcho through heaven;
My soul will respond,
  To Immanuel be given
All glory, all honor,
  All might and dominion,
Who brought us through grace
To the Eden above.

---

### 113.  Evening Praise.

1. SEE, daylight is fading
    O'er earth and o'er ocean,
The sun has gone down
    On the far-distant sea;
Oh now, in the hush
    Of the fitful commotion,
We lift our tired spirits,
    Blest Saviour, to thee.
Full oft wast thou praying
    Alone on the mountain,
As eventide spread
    Her dark wing o'er the wave;
Thou Son of the Highest,
    And life's endless Fountain,
Be with us, we pray thee,
    To bless and to save.

2. And oft as the tumult
    Of life's heaving billow
  Shall toss our frail bark,
    Driving wild o'er night's deep.
  Let thy healing wing
    Be stretched over our pillow,
  And guard us from evil,
    Though Death watch our sleep.
  To God, our great Father,
    Whose throne is in heaven,
  Who dwells with the lowly
    And humble in heart,
  To the Son and the Spirit
    All glory be given ;
  One God, ever blesséd
    And praiséd, thou art.    HEBER

## 114.  The Sheepfold.

1. WHEN Jesus the meek
  And the lowly was here,
    He spoke in the accents of love :
  "Forbid not the children
  To come unto me ;
    Of such is the kingdom above."
  Great Shepherd, I 'm helpless,
    And often I rove ;
  My sins and my follies

In pity remove,
And gather a child
In the arms of thy love,
And give him a place in thy fold.

2. Then in thy green pastures
I'll lay myself down,
And feed on thy life-giving word;
I'll drink of the waters
That peacefully flow,
And never by tempests are stirred.
But guard me and guide me,
My Shepherd, I pray,
And give me a heart
Thy commands to obey,
To turn from temptation
And tempters away,
And never depart from thy fold.

3. Oh why on the mountains
So cold and so drear,
Where darkness and dangers appal,
Should children be suffered
To wander and die,
When Jesus would welcome them all?
Ye friends of the children,
Go gather them in,
And study to woo them,

And labor to win.
Before they are wedded
To folly and sin
And die far away from the fold.

4. For 't is not the will
Of the Shepherd divine,
That one of these lambs should be lost ;
A precious salvation
He purchased for them,
And tongue cannot tell what it cost :
He grieves when he sees them
By folly beguiled,
For precious to him
Is the soul of a child,
And safely at last,
In the land undefiled,
He gathers them into his fold.     ▲ ▲ ◎.

---

## 115. Wandering Lambs.

1. OVER the mountains, barren and cold,
Far from the pasture, far from the fold,
Wander the lambs, by folly beguiled ;
Rescue the children, friends of the child.

### CHORUS.

Hasten to seek them, hasten to save,
Ere they be lost in the night of the grave.

131

2. Jesus the Shepherd loves to behold
Lambs of his flock secure in his fold;
Grieved is the heart of infinite Love,
When from the sheepfold little ones rove.
CHORUS—Hasten to seek, etc.

3 Pleasures allure them, false as they're fair;
Lies in their pathway many a snare,
Tempters around them seek to decoy,
Dangers in ambush wait to destroy.

4. Gently and kindly guide the young feet,
Line upon line, with patience entreat;
Happy the heart whose labor is this—
Guiding a child to mansions of bliss.

A. A. G.

## 116.  The Dewdrop.

1. How small are the dewdrops,
      Those gems of the morning,
That bathe with effulgence
      The field and the flower;
How transient their stay
      And how brief their adorning,
How humble their mission—
      To shine for an hour;
But think of them rightly,
Don't speak of them lightly,

Because you can brush them
By thousands away ;
Though drops when they 're single,
They 're streams when they mingle
And run with the rivers
Away to the sea.

2. So gifts from the youthful,
Their prayers and their labors,
Like dew on the flowers,
May but trifles appear ;
But blend the bright drop
With its glistening neighbors,
And streams of refreshment
The desert shall cheer.
Then, children, do n't falter,
But bring to the altar
The word kindly spoken,
The mite, or the tear :
For grains make the mountain,
And drops make the fountain,
And moments united
Will compass a year.

3. Then ever be doing
And ever devising ;
Do n't say, "I 'm a child,
I will work when a man ;"

133

The season of small things
　Be never despising,
But fill up your measure,
　And do what you can.
Do n't ever be hoarding,
And riches applauding ;
Keep giving, and you
　Shall have plenty to give :
The truest enjoyment
Is found in employment ;
For God and humanity
　Labor and live.　　　　▲. ▲. ▲.

------◆------

### 117.　The Lamb of God.

1. Not all the blood of beasts
　On Jewish altars slain,
Could give the guilty conscience peace,
　Or wash away the stain.

2. But Christ, the heavenly Lamb,
　Takes all our sins away ;
A sacrifice of nobler name,
　And richer blood than they.

3. My faith would lay her hand
　On that dear head of thine,
While like a penitent I stand,
　And there confess my sin.

4. My faith looks back to see
   The burdens thou didst bear,
When hanging on th' accursed tree,
   And hopes her guilt was there.

5. Believing, we rejoice
   To see the curse remove :
We bless the Lamb with cheerful voice,
   And sing his bleeding love.　WATTS.

## 118.　The Lord is Come.

1. Joy to the world, the Lord is come !
   Let earth receive her King ;
Let every heart prepare him room,
   And heaven and nature sing.

2. Joy to the earth, the Saviour reigns !
   Let men their songs employ ;
While fields and floods, rocks, hills, and plains,
   Repeat the sounding joy.

3. No more let sins and sorrows grow,
   Nor thorns infest the ground :
He comes to makes his blessings flow
   Far as the curse is found.

4. He rules the world with truth and grace,
   And makes the nations prove
The glories of his righteousness,
   And wonders of his love.　WATTS.

135

## 119.   Praise to Christ.

1. OH for a thousand tongues to sing
   My dear Redeemer's praise ;
   The glories of my God and King,
   The triumphs of his grace.

2. Jesus, the name that calms our fears,
   That bids our sorrow cease ;
   'T is music to our ravished ears ;
   'T is life and health and peace.

3. He breaks the power of reigning sin,
   He sets the pris'ner free ;
   His blood can make the foulest clean—
   His blood availed for me.           WESLEY

## 120.   Latter-day Glory.

1. BEHOLD, the mountain of the Lord
   In latter days shall rise
   Above the mountains and the hills,
   And draw the wondering eyes.

2. To this the joyful nations round,
   All tribes and tongues shall flow ;
   "Up to the hill of God," they say,
   "And to his courts we'll go."

136

3. The beams that shine on Zion's hill
   Shall lighten every land ;
The King who reigns in Salem's towers
   Shall all the world command.

4. No longer hosts encountering hosts
   Their millions slain deplore ;
They hang the trumpet in the hall,
   And study war no more.

5. Come then, Oh come from every land,
   To worship at his shrine ;
And walking in the light of God,
   With holy beauties shine.    LOGAN

-----------·-----------

## 121. Nothing but Leaves !

1. NOTHING but leaves ; the Spirit grieves
   Over a wasted life,
O'er sin committed while conscience slept,
Promises made but never kept,
   Folly and shame and strife,
Nothing but leaves ! nothing but leaves !

2 Nothing but leaves ; no ripened sheaves
   Garnered of life's fair grain :
We sow our seed—lo, tares and weeds,
Words, idle words for earnest deeds ;
   Reaping, we find with pain
Nothing but leaves ! nothing but leaves !

3. Nothing but leaves : and memory weaves
   No veil to hide the past ;
And as we trace our weary way
Counting each lost and misspent day,
   Sadly we find at last
Nothing but leaves! nothing but leaves!

4 And shall we meet the Master so,
   Bearing our withered leaves?
The Saviour looks for perfect fruit ;
Stand we before him sad and mute,
   Waiting the word he breathes,
   "Nothing but leaves! nothing but leaves!

---

## 122.  Jesus Reigns.

1. Hark! ten thousand harps and voices
   Sound the notes of praise above ;
Jesus reigns, and heaven rejoices ;
   Jesus reigns, the God of love :
See, he sits on yonder throne ;
Jesus rules the world alone :
      CHORUS.
   Hallelujah! hallelujah!
   Hallelujah! Amen.

2. Jesus hail! whose glory brightens
   All above and gives it worth ;
Lord of life, thy smile enlightens,
   Cheers, and charms thy saints on earth :
138

When we think of love like thine,
Lord, we own it love divine.
CHORUS—Hallelujah, etc.

3. King of glory, reign for ever—
  Thine an everlasting crown :
Nothing from thy love shall sever
  Those whom thou hast made thine own ·
Happy objects of thy grace,
Destined to behold thy face.

4. Saviour, hasten thine appearing ;
  Bring, Oh bring the glorious day,
When, the awful summons hearing,
  Heaven and earth shall pass away :
Then with golden harps we 'll sing,
  "Glory, glory to our King." KELLY.

## 123. Light in Darkness.

1. LIGHT of those whose dreary dwelling
  Borders on the shades of death,
Rise on us, thyself revealing—
  Rise and chase the clouds beneath.
Thou, of heaven and earth Creator,
  In our deepest darkness rise ;
Scatter all the night of nature,
  Pour the day upon our eyes.

2. Still we wait for thine appearing;
    Life and joy thy beams impart,
Chasing all our fears, and cheering
    Every meek, benighted heart.
By thine all-sufficient merit,
    Every burdened soul release ;
Every weary, wandering spirit
    Guide into thy perfect peace.

## 124. Send the Tidings.

1. SEND the tidings of salvation
    To the heathen sunk in sin :
All without is desolation,
    All is wretchedness within.

### CHORUS.

||:Send the tidings, send the tidings,
    Jesus died the lost to save. :||

2. While the light is round you shining,
    Pointing out the narrow path,
Heathen in their darkness pining,
    Walk the downward road to wrath.
    CHORUS—Send the tidings, etc.

3. When in sorrow's hour you languish,
    Some sweet promise cheers your heart;
They, thro' days and nights of anguish,
    Nothing find to ease the smart.

140

4. On the Saviour's bosom lying,
    You can smile when death draws near,
But the heathen, when he's dying,
    Sinks in darkness and despair.

5. Think upon their desolation,
    Pray and toil their souls to save ;
Send the gospel of salvation,
    Ere they moulder in the grave. ·▲ ▲ ◖

---

### 125. Missionary Hymn.

1. From Greenland's icy mountains,
    From India's coral strand,
Where Afric's sunny fountains
    Roll down their golden sand ;
From many an ancient river,
    From many a palmy plain,
They call us to deliver
    Their land from error's chain.

2. What though the spicy breezes
    Blow soft o'er Ceylon's isle,
Though every prospect pleases,
    And only man is vile ;
In vain with lavish kindness
    The gifts of God are strown,
The heathen in his blindness
    Bows down to wood and stone.

141

3. Shall we, whose souls are lighted
   With wisdom from on high,
Shall we to men benighted
   The lamp of life deny?
Salvation! Oh, salvation!
   The joyful sound proclaim,
Till earth's remotest nation
   Has learned Messiah's name.

4. Waft, waft, ye winds, his story,
   And you, ye waters, roll,
Till, like a sea of glory,
   It spreads from pole to pole;
Till o'er our ransomed nature
   The Lamb, for sinners slain,
Redeemer, King, Creator,
   In bliss returns to reign.     HEBER.

———————◆———————

## 126. Morning Light.

1. THE morning light is breaking,
   The darkness disappears.
The sons of earth are waking
   To penitential tears:
Each breeze that sweeps the ocean
   Brings tidings from afar
Of nations in commotion,
   Prepared for Zion's war.

2. See heathen nations bending
   Before the God we love,
   And thousand hearts ascending
   In gratitude above ;
   While sinners now confessing,
   The gospel call obey,
   And seek the Saviour's blessing--
   A nation in a day.

3. Blest river of salvation,
   Pursue thy onward way,
   Flow thou to every nation,
   Nor in thy richness stay ;
   Stay not, till all the lowly
   Triumphant reach their home ;
   Stay not, till all the holy
   Proclaim, "The Lord has come."

S. F. SMITH.

### 127. The Lord's Anointed.

1. HAIL to the Lord's Anointed,
   Great David's greater Son ;
   Hail, in the time appointed,
   His reign on earth begun !
   He comes to break oppression,
   To set the captive free ;
   To take away transgression,
   And rule in equity.

2. He comes with succor speedy
     To those who suffer wrong,
   To help the poor and needy,
     And bid the weak be strong ;
   To give them songs for sighing,
     Their darkness turn to light,
   Whose souls, condemned and dying,
     Were precious in his sight.

3. For him shall prayer unceasing
     And daily vows ascend ;
   His kingdom still increasing,
     A kingdom without end :
   The tide of time shall never
     His covenant remove ;
   His name shall stand for ever,
     That name to us is LOVE.

MONTGOMERY.

## 128.   The Gospel Banner.

1. Now be the gospel banner
     In every land unfurled,
   And be the shout Hosanna
     Reëchoed through the world :
   Till every isle and nation,
     Till every tribe and tongue,
   Receive the great salvation,
     And join the happy throng.

2. Yes, thou shalt reign for ever,
    O Jesus, King of kings!
Thy light, thy love, thy favor
    Each ransomed captive sings :
The isles for thee are waiting,
    The deserts learn thy praise,
The hills and valleys greeting,
    The song responsive raise.

## 129. Latter-Day.

1. GLORIOUS things of thee are spoken,
    Zion, city of our God ;
He whose word cannot be broken,
    Formed thee for his own abode :
On the Rock of ages founded,
    What can shake thy sure repose ?
With salvation's walls surrounded,
    Thou mayest smile at all thy foes.

2. See the streams of living waters,
    Springing from eternal love,
Well supply thy sons and daughters,
    And all fear of want remove.
Who can faint while such a river
    Ever flows their thirst t' assuage ?
Grace which, like the Lord, the giver
    Never fails from age to age.

3. Round each habitation hovering,
   See the cloud and fire appear,
For a glory and a covering,
   Showing that the Lord is near.
Thus deriving from their banner
   Light by night and shade by day,
Safe they feed upon the manna
   Which he gives them when they pray

## 130.  Good Tidings.

1. SHOUT the tidings of salvation
   To the aged and the young,
Till the precious invitation
   Waken every heart and tongue ;
Shout the tidings of salvation
   O'er the prairies of the west,
Till each gathering congregration,
   With the gospel sound is blest.

2. Shout the tidings of salvation,
   Mingling with the ocean's roar,
Till the ships of every nation
   Bear the news from shore to shore ;
Shout the tidings of salvation
   O'er the islands of the sea,
Till, in humble adoration,
   All to Christ shall bow the knee.

## 131.  Little Things.

1. LITTLE drops of water
     Little grains of sand,
   Make the mighty ocean
     And the beauteous land.

2. And the little moments,
     Humble though they be,
   Make the mighty ages
     Of eternity.

3. So our little errors
     Lead the soul away
   From the paths of virtue,
     Oft in sin to stray.

4. Little deeds of kindness,
     Little words of love,
   Make our earth an Eden
     Like the heaven above.

5 Little seeds of mercy,
     Sown by youthful hands,
   Grow to bless the nations
     Far in heathen lands.

## 132.  Praise to Christ.

1. JESUS, high in glory,
     Lend a listening ear;
   When we bow before thee,
     Infant praises hear.

2. We are little children,
   Weak and apt to stray ;
   Saviour, guide and keep us
   In the heavenly way.

3. Save us, Lord, from sinning,
   Watch us day by day ;
   Help us now to love thee,
   Take our sins away.

4. Then, when Jesus calls us
   To our heavenly home,
   We will answer gladly,
   "Saviour, Lord, we come."

## 133. Go Work To-Day.

1. THERE's a voice in the air,
   A still small voice,
And it comes to our ear while we play ;
   In the morning it comes,
      Though we heed not the sound,
   And at noon and at evening
      It follows us round :
‖: "Go work in my vineyard to-day." :‖

2. 'T is the voice of our Father,
   From heaven it comes,
And it finds us wherever we stray ;
   In the field or the town.

In the house or the street,
Whether welcome or not,
The same accents we meet:
‖: " Go work in my vineyard to-day.":‖

3. 'T is our Father who calls;
He calls us in love;
Let us hasten that call to obey:
He has given us life
And each good we enjoy;
Let us then for his love
All our efforts employ;
‖:" We 'll work in his vineyard to-day. :‖

4. All blessings come down
From his throne in the sky;
All he asks is that we should obey:
He has saved us from death;
When life's journey shall end,
He will love us for ever,
Our Saviour and Friend;
‖:We 'll work in his vineyard to-day. :‖

## 134. I Love a Little Child.

L I love a little child with his sparkling eye,
And his cheek like the blushing rose;
I love his merry laugh and his sunny face,
When the joy of the heart o'erflows.

CHORUS.

Happy little children,
With cares light and few,
In the loving heart you 'll find
A warm place for you.

2. I love a little child
With her step so light,
As she glides like a spirit by ;
I love her gentle mirth
And her soft sweet songs,
Which with birds of the wild-wood vie.
CHORUS—Happy little children, etc.

3. I love them better yet
When I see them meet
In the school on the Sabbath-day,
To learn their Father's will,
And his praise to sing,
And to walk in the heavenly way.

4. I love them best of all,
When their wayward hearts
Are subdued by a Saviour's love ;
Though now the cross they bear,
Yet the crown they 'll wear
When they pass to their home above.

## 135. Do What You Can.

1. Do n't think there is nothing
   For children to do,
Because they can't work like a man,
   The harvest is great
      And the laborers few :
Then, children, do all that you can.

CHORUS.

Children, do all that you can ;
Children, do all that you can ;
The harvest is great
And the laborers few :
Then, children, do all that you can.

2. You think, if great riches
      You had at command,
Your zeal should no weariness know
      You 'd scatter your wealth
         With a liberal hand,
And succor the children of woe.
         CHORUS—Children, do all, etc.

3. But what if you 've naught
      But a penny to give ?
Then give it, though scanty your store ;
   For those who give nothing
      When little they have,
When wealthy will do little more.

4. It was not the off'ring
   Of pomp and of power,
It was not the golden bequest—
   Ah no, 't was the mite
   From the hand of the poor
That Jesus applauded and blessed.

5. Then do n't be a sluggard
   And live at your ease,
And life with vain pleasures beguile ;
   But ever be active
   And busy as bees,
And God on your labors will smile.

A. A. G

---

## 136. Little Servants.

1. Oh what can little hands, little hands do
   To please the King of heaven ?
The little hands some work may try
To help the poor in misery—
   Such grace to mine be given.

2. Oh what can little lips, little lips do
   To please the King of heaven ?
The little lips can praise and pray,
And gentle words of kindness say—
   Such grace to mine be given.

3. Oh what can little eyes, little eyes do
   To please the King of heaven?
   The little eyes can upward look,
   Can learn to read God's holy book:
   Such grace to mine be given.

4. Oh what can little hearts, little hearts do
   To please the King of heaven?
   The hearts, if God his Spirit send,
   Can love and trust the children's Friend:
   Such grace to mine be given.

5. When hearts and hands and lips unite
   To please the King of heaven,
   And serve the Saviour with delight,
   They are most precious in his sight:
   Such grace to mine be given.

FABER.

## 137. Morning Songs.

1. As the birds in shady wildwood
   Cheer the weary traveller,
   So the songs of blooming childhood
   Cheer the heart oppressed with care.

CHORUS.

‖:Happy voices, happy voices,
   Precious gift from God above. :‖

153

2. Welcome, hour of pure enjoyment,
   When the tuneful band unite
In the heaven approved employment
   Of the ransomed saints in light.

3. Every loving heart rejoices,
   And the angel flight delays;
For 't is sweet when hearts and voices
   Blend in songs of sacred praise.

4. Precious youth, in life's bright morning
   Train ye for the heavenly choir;
From the ways of folly turning,
   To a heavenly harp aspire.      ▲ ▲. ◐

## 138. A Happy Home.

1. I HAVE a home, a happy home,
   And friends who love me there;
With daily bread I still am fed,
   Have still warm clothes to wear:
I've health and strength in every limb,
   How grateful should I be;
How shall I show my love to Him
   Who shows such love to me?

2. While some are blind, or deaf, or lame,
   I hear the sweet birds sing,
Can bound along with joyful song,
   Can watch the flowers of spring;

No wasting pain my eye to dim,
From want and sickness free;
How shall I show my love to Him
Who shows such love to me?

3. And blessings greater still than these
A gracious God has given—
The precious word of Christ our Lord
To guide my feet to heaven.
Among the shining cherubim
I trust my home shall be:
How shall I show my love to Him
Who shows such love to me?

4. My God, I am a feeble child;
Oh teach me to obey,
With humble fear to serve thee here,
To watch and praise and pray:
My love is weak, my faith is dim,
But grace I ask from thee,
That I may prove my love for Him
Who loved and died for me.

## 139. Sunday-School Battle Song.

1. MARCHING on, marching on,
Glad as birds on the wing,
Come the bright ranks of children
From near and from far;

Happy hearts, full of song,
'Neath our banners we bring,
Little soldiers of Zion,
Prepared for the war.

### CHORUS.

Marching on, marching on,
Sound the battle cry, sound the battle cry,
For the Saviour is before us,
And for him we draw the sword :
Marching on, marching on,
Shout the victory, shout the victory !
We will end the battle singing,
"Hallelujah to the Lord.'

2. Pressing on, pressing on
To the din of the fray,
With the firm tread of faith
To the battle we go ;
'Mid the cheering of angels
Our ranks march away,
With our flags pointing ever
Right on towards the foe.
CHORUS—Marching on, etc.

3. Fighting on, fighting on,
In the midst of the strife,
At the call of our Captain
We draw every sword :

We are battling for God.
  We are struggling for life :
Let us strike every rebel
  That fights 'gainst the Lord.

4. Singing on. singing on,
    From the battle we come ;
  Every flag bears a wreath,
    Every soldier renown ;
  Heavenly angels are waiting
    To welcome us home,
  And the Saviour will give us
    A robe and a crown.

---

## 140. Gloria in Excelsis.

1. GLORY be to God on high,
  And on earth peace, good-will towards men.

2. We praise thee, we bless thee, we worship thee,
  We glorify thee, we give thanks to thee for
  thy great glory.

3. For thou only art holy,
  Thou only art the Lord.

4. Thou only, O Christ, with the Holy Ghost,
  Art most high in the glory of God the Father.  Amen.

## 141. Love at Home.

1. THERE is beauty all around,
    When there 's love at home ;
There is joy in every sound,
    When there 's love at home.
Peace and plenty here abide,
Smiling sweet on every side,
Time doth softly, sweetly glide,
    When there 's love at home.

2. In the cottage there is joy,
    When there 's love at home ;
Hate and envy ne'er annoy,
    When there 's love at home.
Roses blossom 'neath our feet,
All the earth's a garden sweet
Making life a bliss complete,
    When there 's love at home.

3. Kindly heaven smiles above,
    When there 's love at home ;
All the earth is filled with love,
    When there 's love at home.
Sweeter sings the brooklet by,
Brighter beams the azure sky ;
Oh, there 's One who smiles on high
    When there 's love at home.

4. Jesus, show thy mercy mine,
   Then there's love at home;
Sweetly whisper, I am thine,
   Then there's love at home.
Source of love, thy cheering light
Far exceeds the sun so bright—
Can dispel the gloom of night;
   Then there's love at home.

---

## 142. I'm a Little Pilgrim.

1. I'm a little pilgrim
     And a stranger here;
   Though this world is pleasant,
     Sin is always near.
   There's a better country,
     Where there is no sin,
   Where the tones of sorrow
     Never enter in.

2. But a little pilgrim
     Must have garments clean,
   If he'd wear the white robes
     And with Christ be seen.
   Jesus, cleanse and save me,
     Teach me to obey;
   Holy Spirit, guide me
     On my heavenly way.

## 143. Little Child's Prayer.

1. JESUS, tender Saviour,
   Hast thou died for me?
Make me very thankful
   In my heart to thee.
When the sad, sad story
   Of thy grief I read,
Make me very sorry
   For my sins indeed.

2. Now I know thou livest,
   And dost plead for me;
Make me very thankful
   In my prayers to thee.
Soon I hope in glory
   At thy side to stand;
Make me meet to see thee
   In that happy land.

## 144. The Good Shepherd.

1. JESUS is our Shepherd,
   Wiping every tear;
Folded in his bosom,
   What have we to fear?
Only let us follow
   Whither he doth lead,
To the thirsty desert,
   Or the dewy mead.

160

2. Jesus is our Shepherd ;
　　Well we know his voice ;
How its gentlest whisper
　　Makes our heart rejoice!
Even when he chideth,
　　Tender is his tone ;
None but he shall guide us,
　　We are his alone.

3. Jesus is our Shepherd,
　　For the sheep he bled ;
Every lamb is sprinkled
　　With the blood he shed.
When we tread death's valley,
　　Dark with fearful gloom,
We will fear no evil,
　　Victors o'er the tomb.

---

## 145. Now the Sabbath Eve Declining.

1. Now the Sabbath eve declining,
　　Sheds around a hallowed light,
And the silver stars are shining
　　With a radiance pure and bright.
Soft and gentle be the numbers
　　Which our grateful spirits raise :
God above, while nature slumbers,
　　Hear, Oh hear our song of praise.

2. May the words of inspiration
   Which our ears have heard to-day,
Wake a holy contemplation,
   Call our souls from earth away.
While with hearts and voices blending,
   Up to heaven our thoughts we raise,
Thou to mortal vows attending,
   Hear, Oh hear our song of praise.

### 146.   God is Near Thee.

1. God is near thee,
   Therefore cheer thee,
     Sad soul ;
   He 'll defend thee
   When around thee
     Billows roll.

2. Calm thy sadness,
   Look in gladness
     On high ;
   Faint and weary,
   Pilgrim, cheer thee,
     Help is nigh.

3. Mark the sea-bird,
   Wildly wheeling
     Through the skies

God defends him,
God attends him
When he cries.

4. God is near thee,
Therefore cheer thee,
Sad soul ;
He 'll defend thee
When around thee
Billows roll.

---

## 147. Memory.

1. WHEN shall we meet again—
Meet, ne'er to sever ?
When shall peace wreathe her chain
Round us for ever ?
Our hearts will ne'er repose,
Safe from each blast that blows,
In this dark world of woes—
Never, no, never.

2. When shall love freely flow,
Pure as life 's river ?
When shall sweet friendship glow
Changeless for ever ?
Where joys celestial thrill,
Where bliss each heart shall fill,
And fears of parting chill—
Never, no, never.

163

3. Up to that world of light,
   Take us, dear Saviour;
May we all there unite,
   Happy for ever;
Where kindred spirits dwell,
There may our music swell,
And time our joys dispel—
   Never, no, never.

4. Soon shall we meet again—
   Meet, ne'er to sever;
Soon will peace wreathe her chain
   Round us for ever:
Our hearts will then repose
Secure from worldly foes;
Our songs of praise shall close—
   Never, no, never.

## 148. Our Own Dear Home.

1 HOME, dear home, we never can forget;
Friends, dear friends, we often there have met;
Pressed by care, or pierced by grief,
Home has afforded us a sweet relief.

CHORUS.

Tender memories round thee twine,
Like the ivy green round the pine;
Over land and sea we may roam,
Still will we cherish thee, our own dear home.

164

2. Lured by gain we seek a foreign shore,
 Worn and weary heap the golden ore;
 Still our yearning hearts demand
 Rest in the homestead in our native land.
  CHORUS—Tender memories, etc.

3. On the gilded page of earthly fame
 Some may pant to register their name;
 Round our names no wreath may be,
 But you may read them on the old home tree.
  CHORUS—Tender memories, etc.

4. Painted pleasure holds the flowing bowl,
 Mirth and music lure the careless soul;
 But with us at home, you'll find
 Home joys that never leave a sting behind.

5. Firmly bound by silver chains of love,
 Here are foretastes of the home above;
 Thou from whom all blessings come,
 Help us to praise thee for a Christian home.

A. A. C

## 149.  A Beautiful Home.

1. THERE's a beautiful home for thee, brother
  A home, a home for thee;
 In that land of bliss where pleasure is,
  There  brother, 's a home for thee.

CHORUS.

A beautiful home for thee, brother,
A beautiful home for thee ;
In that land of bliss where pleasure is,
There, brother, 's a home for thee.

2. There 's a beautiful rest for thee, brother,
A rest, a rest for thee ;
In those mansions above where all is love,
There, brother, 's a rest for thee.
CHORUS—A beautiful rest, etc.

3. There 's a beautiful crown for thee, brother,
A crown, a crown for thee,
When the battle is done, and the victory won,
Our Saviour will give it to thee.
CHORUS—A beautiful crown, etc.

4. There 's a beautiful robe for thee, brother,
A robe, a robe for thee ;
A robe of white, so pure and bright,
A glorious robe for thee.
CHORUS—A beautiful robe, etc.

5. Wilt seek that beautiful home, brother,
That home, that home above ;
In that land of light, where all is bright,
That land where all is love ?

TOPPING

166

## 150. Home in the Skies.

1. WE'RE passing along
   To our home in the skies;
This garb of the pilgrim
   Our Master supplies;
No costly attire
   Worn by kings of the earth
Ever rivalled its whiteness
   Or equalled its worth.

CHORUS.

Home in the skies,
Happy home in the skies;
We're passing along
To our home in the skies.
Then come join our band,
Take the staff in your hand,
And with us pass along
To our home in the skies.

2. The world may allure us
   With promise and smile,
And Satan our garments
   Of white may defile,
And pleasure may knock
   At the door of our heart;
But we'll look unto Jesus
   And bid them depart.

CHORUS—Home in the skies, etc.

3. When weary, we'll lean
    On the arm of our Guide;
When thirsty, we'll drink
    Of the stream by our side;
When hungry, we'll feed
    On the manna around;
And when struck by the foe,
    There's a balm for the wound.

4. And oft in the distance
    Our home we behold,
Its gates made of pearl
    And its courts paved with gold;
Its pastures so fresh
    And its fountains so clear,
While the anthems of praise
    Faintly fall on the ear.        A. A. G.

## 151. Happy Home Above.

1. WE soon shall leave this foreign land,
    And cross the flowing river,
And in our Saviour's presence stand,
    And sing his praise for ever.

CHORUS.

Oh happy home above, Oh happy home above,
Through endless days we'll sing the praise
Of Jesus and his love.

2. No sorrow there; from radiant eyes
No tears of grief are starting;
No sad farewell, no laboring sighs,
When friend from friend is parting.

3. No lurking foe, no hidden snare,
Shall ever more beguile us;
No pleasures false, as well as fair,
Shall ever more defile us.

4. Then, children, now repent, believe,
And walk the path of duty;
Then in the home above you 'll live,
Where reigns immortal beauty.

--------

## 152. The Good Shepherd.

1. The Lord is my Shepherd,
He makes me repose
Where the pastures in beauty are growing,
He leads me afar
From the world and its woes,
Where in peace the still waters are flowing.

2. He strengthens my spirit,
He shows me the path
Where the arms of his love shall enfold me,
And when I walk through
The dark valley of death,
His rod and his staff will uphold me.

169

## 153.  Shepherd of Israel.

1. Oh tell me, Thou life
    And delight of my soul,
Where the flock of thy pasture are feeding ;
    I seek thy protection,
    I need thy control,
I would go where my Shepherd is leading.

2. Oh tell me the place
    Where thy flock are at rest,
Where the noontide will find them reposing ;
    The tempest now rages,
    My soul is distressed,
And the pathway of peace I am losing.

3. Oh why should I stray
    With the flocks of thy foes,
'Mid the desert where now they are roving,
    Where hunger and thirst,
    Where affliction and woes,
And temptations their ruin are proving?

4. Oh when shall my foes
    And my wanderings cease,
And the follies that fill me with weeping?
    Thou Shepherd of Israel,
    Restore me that peace
Thou dost give to the flock thou art keeping

5. A voice from the Shepherd
Now bids thee return
By the way where the footprints are lying :
No longer to wander,
No longer to mourn,
Oh fair one, now homeward be flying.

HASTINGS

## 154. Morning Song.

1. ONCE more, my soul, the rising day
Salutes my waking eyes ;
Once more, my voice, thy tribute pay
To Him who rules the skies.

2. Night unto night his name repeats,
The day renews the sound,
Wide as the heavens on which he sits
To turn the seasons round.

3. 'T is he supports my mortal frame ;
My tongue shall speak his praise ;
My sins would rouse his wrath to flame,
And yet his wrath delays.

4. Great God, let all my hours be thine,
While I enjoy the light ;
Then shall my sun in smiles decline,
And bring a pleasant night.     WATTS

### 155.   The Hope of Heaven.

1. WHEN I can read my title clear
   To mansions in the skies,
   I bid farewell to every fear,
   And wipe my weeping eyes.

2. Should earth against my soul engage,
   And hellish darts be hurled,
   Then I can smile at Satan's rage,
   And face a frowning world.

3. Let cares, like a wild deluge, come,
   And storms of sorrow fall ;
   May I but safely reach my home,
   My God, my heaven, my all—

4. There shall I bathe my weary soul
   In seas of heavenly rest,
   And not a wave of trouble roll
   Across my peaceful breast.         WATTS.

---

### 156.   A Daily Petition.

1. FATHER, whate'er of earthly bliss
   Thy sovereign will denies,
   Accepted at thy throne of grace
   Let this petition rise :

2. "Give me a calm, a thankful heart,
   From every murmur free;
   The blessings of thy grace impart,
   And let me live to thee.

3. "Let the sweet hope that I am thine
   My life and death attend;
   Thy presence through my journey shine,
   And crown my journey's end." STEELE.

## 157. Jerusalem Above.

1. JERUSALEM, my happy home,
   Name ever dear to me,
   When shall my labors have an end
   In joy and peace and thee?

2. When shall these eyes thy heaven-built walls
   And pearly gates behold,
   Thy bulwarks with salvation strong,
   And streets of shining gold?

3. Oh when, thou city of my God,
   Shall I thy courts ascend,
   Where congregations ne'er break up,
   And Sabbaths have no end?

4. There happier bowers than Eden bloom,
   Nor sin, nor sorrow know:
   Blest seats, through rude and stormy scenes
   I onward press to you.

5. Jerusalem, my happy home
My soul still pants for thee;
Then shall my labors have an end
When I thy joys shall see. c. WESLEY.

## 158.   Christmas Hymn.

1. CHRIST is born, and heaven rejoices,
Judah's plain is bathed in light;
Thousand, thousand harps and voices
Break the silence of the night.
CHORUS.
‖:Glory in the highest, glory,
Peace on earth, good-will to men.:‖

2. Christ is born, the Lord's Anointed
Leaves the heavenly world awhile,
Enters on the work appointed,
God' and man to reconcile.
CHORUS—Glory in the highest, etc.

3. To the lost he brings salvation,
Freedom to the captive slave;
Peace amid death's desolation,
Victory o'er the boasting grave.

4. Christ is born, Oh wondrous story!
Lord of life, yet born to die;
Sorrow's child, yet King of glory;
Born to rule and reign on high.
174

5. Royal babe, though few enthrone him,
    Few their grateful offerings bring,
All the tribes of earth shall own him
    Prince of peace, creation's King.   ᴀ ᴀ. ᴏ

---

## 159.   Star of Bethlehem.

1. Saw you never in the twilight,
    When the sun has left the skies,
Up in heaven the clear stars shining
    Through the gloom like silver eyes?
So of old, the wise men watching,
    Saw a little stranger star,
And they knew the King was given,
    And they followed it from far.

2. Heard you never of the story
    How they crossed the desert wild,
Journeyed on by plain and mountain,
    Till they found the holy Child—
How they opened all their treasure,
    Kneeling to that infant King,
Gave the gold and fragrant incense,
    Gave the myrrh in offering?

3. Know you not that lowly infant
    Was the bright and Morning Star,
He who came to light the Gentiles
    And the darkened isles afar?

**175**

And we too may seek his cradle,
   There our hearts' best treasure bring;
Love and faith and true devotion,
   For our Saviour, God, and King.

## 160. Christmas Song.

1. THE city's hum was hushed and still,
And silence reigned o'er vale and hill;
The birds had sought the sheltering tree,
The flocks were folded tenderly;
No sound of life was on the breeze,
That murmured through the olive-trees,
And 'mid the stars heaven's brightest gem
Shone over sleeping Bethlehem:

CHORUS.

Good tidings, good tidings,
   Good tidings of great joy!
On this blest morn a Prince is born!
   Good tidings of great joy!
The Prince of peace, the Incarnate Word,
A Saviour, Christ the Lord!
   Glory to God in the highest, then,
Glory to God in the highest,
   And on earth peace, good-will to men.

2. In rapturous tones that strain arose,
And burst upon the night's repose;

A white-winged legion from on high
With dazzing glory filled the sky:
The music of the angel band
Went floating o'er the Holy Land,
While on the listening shepherds' ear
Still rang that chorus loud and clear—
   CHORUS—Good tidings, etc.

3 The vision faded from the sight,
Hushed were those voices of the night,
And brightly dawned upon the earth
The morning of our Saviour's birth:
Oh morn of gladness, day of joy,
Well may thy praise our tongues employ!
Well may we join that song of love
First sung by minstrels from above.
   CHORUS—Good tidings, etc.   S. H. THAYER.

## 161. Christmas Carol.

1. WE three kings of Orient are;
Bearing gifts we traverse afar
    Field and fountain,
    Moor and mountain,
Following yonder star.

### CHORUS.
Oh star of wonder, star of night,
Star with royal beauty bright,

Westward leading,
Still proceeding,
Guide us to the perfect Light.

2. Born a King on Bethlehem's plain,
Gold I bring to crown him again—
King for ever,
Ceasing never
Over us all to reign.
CHORUS—Oh star of wonder, etc.

3. Frankincense to offer have I:
Incense owns a deity nigh;
Prayer and praising
All men raising,
Worship him God on high.
CHORUS—Oh star of wonder, etc.

4. Myrrh is mine: its bitter perfume
Breathes a life of gathering gloom—
Sorrowing, sighing,
Bleeding, dying,
Sealed in the stone-cold tomb.

5. Glorious now behold him arise,
King and God and Sacrifice;
Heaven singing
Hallelujah;
Joyous the earth replies.

178

## 162. Seeking Christ's Care.

1. SAVIOUR, listen to our prayer,
Poor and sinful though we are ;
Guilt-confessing,
Give thy blessing,
Grant us thy loving care.

CHORUS.

O God our Father, Christ our King,
Now to thee our hearts we bring ;
Keep them ever,
Blessed Saviour,
Till in heaven thy love we sing.

2. Strength is thine ; we often stray
From thy pure and holy way ;
Wilt thou guide us,
Walk beside us,
Nearer every day?
CHORUS—O God our Father. etc.

3. Then may we, when life is o'er,
Stand with thee on yonder shore.
Freed from sinning,
Heaven winning,
Praising evermore.
CHORUS—O God our Father, etc.

## 163. Angels' Welcome.

1. My home is in heaven,
   My rest is not here,
Then why should I murmur
   When trials appear?
Be hushed, my dark spirit,
   The worst that can come
But shortens my journey
   And hastens me home.

CHORUS.

Then the angels will come,
   With their music will come,
With music, sweet music
   To welcome me home;
In the bright gates of crystal
   The shining ones will stand,
And sing me a welcome
   To their own native land.

2. It is not for me
   To be seeking my bliss,
And building my hopes
   In a region like this;
I look for a city
   Which hands have not piled,
I pant for a country
   By sin undefiled.

CHORUS—Then the angels, etc.

3. The thorn and the thistle
   Around me may grow;
   I would not recline
   Upon roses below;
   I ask not my portion,
   I seek not my rest
   Till I find them for ever
   On Jesus' own breast.

## 164. "He is Risen."

1. "HE is risen, he is not here;
   Seek him not among the dead.
   He is living, do not fear,"
   So the white-robed angel said.
   He hath conquered every foe,
   He hath shown his power to save,
   When he took the sting from death
   And the victory from the grave.

### CHORUS.

Then with one heart and voice
Let all the earth rejoice;
Let all the living join the strain,
And angels shout it back again:
The Lord is risen, the Lord is risen!
Rejoice, rejoice, rejoice, rejoice!

2. He is risen, he is not here,
  On the earth he walks no more;
All his trials, all his toils,
  All his grief and shame are o'er;
All his purpose is fulfilled,
  All his work on earth is done:
He whom sinners put to death
  Sitteth on the great white throne.
    Chorus—Then with one heart, etc.

3. He is risen, he is not here—
  Not indeed to mortal eyes:
But we all who die with him,
  Shall again with him arise.
'Tis in him alone we live;
  And because he lives again—
Blessed promise, glorious hope!
  We shall with him live and reign.
    B. H. THAYER.

## 165. Morning Hymn.

1. Now the shades of night are gone,
Now the morning light is come;
Lord, we would be thine to-day;
Drive the shades of sin away.

2. Fill our souls with heavenly light
Banish doubt and clear our sight:
In thy service, Lord, to-day,
Help us labor, help us pray.

3 Keep our wayward passions bound,
  Save us from our foes around;
  Going out and coming in,
  Keep us safe from every sin.

4 When our work of life is past,
  Oh receive us all at last;
  Sin's dark night shall be no more
  When we reach the heavenly shore.

HART. COLL.

## 166. Sabbath Morning.

1. CHRIST the Lord is risen to-day,
   Sons of men and angels say:
   Raise your joys and triumphs high,
   Sing, ye heavens, and earth reply.

2. Love's redeeming work is done,
   Fought the fight, the victory won:
   Jesus' agony is o'er,
   Darkness veils the earth no more.

3. Vain the stone, the watch, the seal;
   Christ has burst the gates of hell;
   Death in vain forbids him rise,
   Christ has opened paradise.

4. Lives again our glorious King!
"Where, O death, is now thy sting?"
Once he died our souls to save;
"Where's thy victory, boasting grave?"

CUDWORTH.

## 167. Evening Aspirations.

1. SOFTLY now the light of day
Fades upon my sight away;
Free from care, from labor free,
Lord, I would commune with thee.

2. Soon for me the light of day
Shall for ever pass away;
Then, from sin and sorrow free,
Take me, Lord, to dwell with thee.

DOANE.

## 168. Pilgrim Song.

1. A FEW more years shall roll,
A few more seasons come,
And we shall be with those that rest
Asleep within the tomb.
Then, O my Lord, prepare
My soul for that great day;
Oh wash me in thy precious blood,
And take my sins away.

184

2. A few more suns shall set
   O'er these dark hills of time ;
   And we shall be where suns are not—
   A far serener clime.
   Then, O my Lord, prepare
   My soul for that blest day ;
   Oh wash me in thy precious blood,
   And take my sins away.

3. A few more storms shall beat
   On this wild rocky shore ;
   And we shall be where tempests cease,
   And surges swell no more.
   Then, O my Lord, prepare
   My soul for that calm day ;
   .Oh wash me in thy precious blood,
   And take my sins away.

4. A few more struggles here,
   A few more partings o'er,
   A few more toils, a few more tears,
   And we shall weep no more.
   Then, O my Lord, prepare
   My soul for that blest day ;
   Oh wash me in thy precious blood,
   And take my sins away.

5. A few more Sabbaths here
   Shall cheer us on our way ;
   And we shall reach the endless rest,
   The eternal Sabbath-day.

Then, O my Lord, prepare
My soul for that sweet day;
Oh wash me in thy precious blood,
And take my sins away.

6. 'T is but a little while
And He shall come again,
Who died that we might live, who lives
That we with Him may reign.
Then, O my Lord, prepare
My soul for that glad day;
Oh wash me in thy precious blood,
And take my sins away.     BONAR.

## 169. My Heavenly Home.

1. THIS world is not my home, I know,
For sin and sorrow wound me;
But mercy tempers every blow,
And goodness smiles around me.

CHORUS.

Then let my lot be what it may,
Come gladness, or come sorrow,
I'm nearer to my home to-day,
And may be there to-morrow.

2. The tear may fall, the heart may bleed,
And all look dark and dreary;
But love divine supplies my need,
And cheers the spirit weary.

186

3. As falls the leaf when touched by frost
   So loved ones fall around me ;
   But 't is by mercy's hand are loosed
   The ties that fondly bound me.

4. With heart resigned, I bid adieu
   To those who love, but leave me ;
   My home, my heavenly home's in view,
   Where death shall ne'er bereave me.

5. My heavenly home, where Jesus reigns !
   When I behold thy glory,
   I 'll walk thy ever-verdant plains,
   And sing redemption's story.   A. A. G.

### 170. A Happy New-Year to Thee.

1. A HAPPY New-year to thee, father,
   A happy New-Year to thee !
   Oh, could I thy portion appoint, father,   '
   How blessed that portion should be.
   Thy pathway I'd strew with bright flowers,
       father,
   And wing every moment with joy ;
   No sorrow should ruffle thy brow, father,
   No cankering care should annoy.

2. A happy New-year to thee, mother,
   A happy New-year to thee !
   I think of thy toils and thy tears, mother,
   And moved by love's eloquent plea.

My study shall daily be this, mother:
    To lessen the tears that may start,
To lighten the toils that oppress, mother
    And kindle the joy of thy heart.

3. A happy New-year to thee, brother,
    A happy New-year to thee ;
The future is closed to the eye, brother,
    And we will not wish for the key ;
But joy shall be blended with joy, brother,
    If smoothly we glide through the year ;
If walking the valley of grief, brother,
    Then tear shall be mingled with tear.

4. A happy New-year to thee, sister,
    A happy New-year to thee ;
May grief never dim the bright eye, sister
    That beams with affection for me ;
Through sunshine and showers of the past,
        sister,
    Our hearts and our homes have been one ;
And love burning bright to the last, sister,
    Shall garnish the hours as they run.  A. A. G.

## 171. Thanksgiving.

1. PRAISE the Lord who reigns above,
    And keeps his courts below ;
Praise him for his boundless love,
    And all his greatness show :
188

Praise him for his noble deeds;
    Praise him for his matchless power;
Him from whom all good proceeds,
    Let earth and heaven adore.

2. Publish, spread to all around
    The great Immanuel's name;
Let the gospel trumpet sound;
    The Prince of peace proclaim.
Praise him, every tuneful string;
    All the reach of heavenly art,
All the power of music bring,
    The music of the heart.

3. Him in whom they move and live,
    Let every creature sing;
Glory to our Saviour give,
    And homage to our King.
Hallowed be his name beneath,
    As in heaven, on earth adored;
Praise the Lord in every breath—
    Let all things praise the Lord.

## 172. Thanks and Praise.

1 MEET and right it is to sing,
    In every time and place,
Glory to our heavenly King,
    The God of truth and grace.

Join we then with sweet accord,
   All in one thanksgiving join;
Holy, holy, holy Lord,
   Eternal praise be thine.

2. Thee the first-born sons of light,
   In choral symphonies,
Praise by day, day without night,
   And never, never cease:
Angels and archangels, all
   Praise the sacred Three in One;
Sing and stop, and gaze and fall,
   O'erwhelmed before thy throne.

3 Father, God, thy love we praise
   Which gave thy Son to die;
Jesus, full of truth and grace,
   Alike we glorify;
Spirit, Comforter divine,
   Praise by all to thee be given,
Till we in full chorus join,
   And earth is turned to heaven.

## 173. Gone, Gone.

1. GONE, gone, loved one,
   Gone from our home;
God hath recalled thee
   In thy youthful bloom:

Death's icy fingers
  Rest upon thee now;
Still beauty lingers
  On thy pallid brow.

2. Gone, gone, loved one,
  Gone to thy tomb;
But 't is not cheerless,
  Hope dispels its gloom:
While we are weeping
  O'er the hallowed ground,
Thou art but sleeping
  Till the trump shall sound.

3. Gone, gone, loved one,
  Gone to the blest;
Earth had its pleasures,
  But 't was not thy rest:
Sin and temptation
  Were thy sorrow *here*,
Then full salvation
  Is thy portion *there*.　　A A G

———————•———————

## 174.  O'er the Flowing River.

O'ER the flowing river,
  Little children stand,
Free from sin for ever,
  Happy in that land.

Fairer than the summer flower
Is every holy one,
Singing, shining ever more,
With glory but begun.

2. Once their eyes were streaming
With the tears of woe ;
Now with rapture beaming,
Not a tear they know :
Crowns of glory now they wear,
And ever as they rove,
O'er the tuneful harps they bear
Their skilful fingers move.

3. 'T was Immanuel sought them,
Straying from the fold ;
With a price he bought them,
Dearer far than gold ;
Not the treasures of the mine,
Not bleating flocks he gave ;
Blood he shed—'t was blood divine,
To sanctify and save.

4. Little saints in glory,
Guilty though I be,
I have learned the story,
"Jesus died for me."

192

Ransomed by his blood divine,
My Saviour I will love ;
Bear his cross, then rise and join
Your shining band above.    A. A. G

---

## 175. The Lord's Prayer. Chant.

1. Our Father, which art in heaven, | hallowed |
   be thy | name : |
   Thy kingdom come, thy will be done on |
   earth, as it | is in | heaven :

2. Give us this | day our | daily | bread ;
   And forgive us our trespasses, as we forgive |
   them that | trespass a- | gainst us ;

3. And lead us not into temptation, but de- | liv-
   er | us from | evil ;
   For thine is the kingdom, and the power,
   and the glory, for | ever. | A- | men.

---

## 176. The Little Graves.

1. On the green grass waves
   O'er the silent graves,
   Where the loved and the lost we lay ;
   And you shed a tear
   As you linger here,
   At the close of a summer day.

As you look around
O'er the hallowed ground,
Little graves here and there you see;
And they seem to say,
As you thither stray,
"There's a grave in this ground for thee."

2. In your youthful prime
In your sweet spring time,
You may sink in the silent tomb;
Though your cheek now glows
Like the blushing rose,
Death may steal all its radiant bloom;
And the bell may toll
For a youthful soul
Fled away to the God who gave;
While the mouldering clay
From the light of day
Shall be hid in the cold, cold grave.

3. Oh, be wise to-day,
Nor presume to say
To the voice that would woo and win,
"Go thy way this time,
'T is my youthful prime;
When I'm old I will turn from sin."
Shun the downward path,
For it leads to wrath;

194

While a child to the Saviour fly;
   And the tears they shed
   O'er your earthy bed
Shall be turned into joy on high.   A. A G

---

## 177. A Young Christian's Burial.

1. COME, children, kindly gather
   Round this form beloved,
Whence so soon our heavenly Father
   Hath the soul removed.
Soul, leave the body mortal
   Safe with us at rest,
Pass beyond the golden portal
   To thy Saviour's breast.

CHORUS.
Bright angels, happy spirits,
   Watch with star-like eyes
O'er the spot whence at Christ's summons
   His beloved shall rise.

2. Eyes full of love and gladness,
   Quiet now in sleep,
Closed on all our sin and sadness,
   Never more to weep—
Unclose now with bliss amazing
   In the realms of peace;
Burst to sight, with rapture gazing
   On the Saviour's face.

3. Hark, 'mid the radiant dawning,
    Where night comes no more,
Sweet-toned bells of Sabbath morning
    Sound from that far shore ;
Lo, cherub forms that hover,
    Bearing thee away ;
So farewell, thy night is over,
    Lost in endless day.

## 178.  A Hymn of Praise.

1. GLORY to the Father give—
    Praise him and adore,
God in whom we move and live—
    Praise him ever more.
Children's prayers he deigns to hear—
    Praise him and adore ;
Children's songs delight his ear—
    Praise him ever more.

CHORUS.

Praise, glory, honor, blessing
    To the King of heaven—
Father, Son, and Holy Spirit,
    Be for ever given.

2. Glory to the Son we bring—
    Praise him and adore,
Christ, our Prophet, Priest, and King—
    Praise him ever more.

Children, raise your sweetest strain –
　Praise him and adore ;
To the Lamb, for he was slain—
　Praise him ever more.

3. Glory to the Holy Ghost—
　Praise him and adore ;
He reclaims the sinner lost—
　Praise him ever more.
Children's minds doth he inspire—
　Praise him and adore ;
Touch their tongues with holy fire—
　Praise him ever more.

## 179. Stand Up for Jesus.

1. This life is a battle
　'Gainst Satan and sin,
And we are the soldiers
　The victory to win,
And Christ is the Captain
　Of our little band ;
Whatever opposes,
　For him we will stand.
　　CHORUS.
Then stand up for Jesus,
　Whatever befall ;
On Calvary's mountain
　He stood for us all ;

Then stand up for Jesus,
Stand up for Jesus,
Stand up for Jesus, for Jesus.

2. To God for our armor
　　We'll fail not to go,
He'll clothe us with truth
　　And with righteousness too;
The "gospel of peace"
　　Shall our footsteps attend,
And the good "shield of faith"
　　From all harm shall defend.

3. Salvation our helmet,
　　The Bible our sword,
Though wily our foes,
　　We are "strong in the Lord;"
While watching and praying
　　Our armor keeps bright,
Our Jesus will help us
　　To stand for the right.

4. Though little temptations—
　　The worst ones of all—
Will often beset us
　　To make us to fall,
We'll stand up for Jesus;
　　And when life is o'er,
For us he'll be standing
　　On Jordan's bright shore.

## 180. The New Jerusalem.

1. WE are on our journey home,
   Where Christ our Lord is gone;
   We shall meet around his throne
   ||:When he makes his people one
   In the new Jerusalem. :||

2. We can see that distant home,
   Though clouds roll dark between;
   Faith views the radiant dome,
   ||:And a lustre flashes keen
   From the new Jerusalem. :||

3. Oh glory shining far
   From the never-setting sun;
   Oh trembling morning star,
   ||:Our journey's almost done
   To the new Jerusalem. :||

4. Our hearts are breaking now
   Those mansions fair to see;
   O Lord, thy heavens bow,
   ||:And raise us up with thee
   To the new Jerusalem. :||

## 181. The Still Small Voice.

1. OFT as I rove, in thoughtless mood,
   Along life's flowery, sunny road,
   Unconscious how the path may end,
   Unheeding where my footsteps tend,

I hear a voice which seems to say,
In a gentle whisper, Come away, Come away!
Softly it whispers, Come away, Come away,
Come away!

2. From day to day that voice I hear,
And oftenest when no friend is near—
When on some secret purpose bent,
Or on some pleasure too intent—
A still small voice which seems to say,
In a gentle whisper, Come away, Come away!
Softly it whispers, Come away, Come away!

3. At times perchance too near I tread
Some cruel quicksand's treacherous bed,
Some yawning gulf, some fatal snare,
Some spot where death is in the air;
Then comes that warning voice to say,
In a gentle whisper, Come away, Come away!
Softly it whispers, Come away, Come away!

4. Some foe with radiant beauty drapes
Temptation in a thousand shapes,
And many a glittering prize is given
To lure me far from home and heaven;
But never fails that voice to say,
With its gentle whisper, Come away, Come
away!
Softly it whispers, Come away, Come away

5. Ah, gentle Spirit, faithful Friend,
Be with me always to life's end,
Till He who keeps my heavenly crown
Shall send his loving angel down,
Upon my brow his hand to lay,
And kindly bid me, Come away, Come away!
And softly whisper, Come away, Come away!

S. H. THAYER.

## 182. Rock of Ages.

1. Rock of ages, cleft for me,
Let me hide myself in thee ;
Let the water and the blood,
From thy riven side that flowed,
Be of sin the double cure,
Cleanse me from its guilt and power.

2. Not the labor of my hands
Can fulfil thy law's demands :
Could my zeal no respite know,
Could my tears for ever flow,
All for sin could not atone ;
Thou must save, and thou alone.

3. Nothing in my hand I bring,
Simply to thy cross I cling ;
Naked, come to thee for dress ;
Helpless, look to thee for grace ;
Vile, I to the fountain fly ;
Wash me, Saviour, or I die!

201

4. While I draw this fleeting breath,
When my eyelids close in death,
When I soar to worlds unknown,
See thee on thy judgment-throne,
Rock of ages, cleft for me,
Let me hide myself in thee.      TOFLADI

## 1S3.   Invitation.

1. FROM the cross uplifted high,
Where the Saviour deigns to die,
What melodious sounds we hear
Bursting on the ravished ear:
"Love's redeeming work is done;
Come and welcome, sinner, come!

2. "Sprinkled now with blood the throne,
Why beneath thy burdens groan?
On thy piercéd body laid,
Justice owns the ransom paid;
Bow the knee, and kiss the Son,
Come and welcome, sinner, come!

3. "Soon the days of life shall end;
Lo, I come, your Saviour, Friend,
Safe your spirits to convey
To the realms of endless day—
Up to my eternal home,
Come and welcome, sinner, come."
202

## 184. Heaven is My Home.

1. I'm but a stranger here,
    Heaven is my home:
Earth is a desert drear,
    Heaven is my home:
Danger and sorrow stand
Round me on every hand;
Heaven is my fatherland,
    Heaven is my home.

2. What though the tempest rage,
    Heaven is my home;
Short is my pilgrimage;
    Heaven is my home;
Time's cold and wintry blast
Soon will be overpast.
I shall reach home at last;
    Heaven is my home.

3. There, at my Saviour's side,
    Heaven is my home;
I shall be glorified,
    Heaven is my home:
There are the good and blest,
Those I love most and best;
There too I soon shall rest,
    Heaven is my home.

## 185. Nearer to Thee.

1. NEARER, my God, to thee,
   Nearer to thee :
   E'en though it be a cross
   That raiseth me ;
   Still all my song shall be,
   Nearer, my God, to thee,
   Nearer to thee.

2. Though like a wanderer,
   Daylight all gone,
   Darkness be over me,
   My rest a stone,
   Yet in my dreams I'd be
   Nearer, my God, to thee,
   Nearer to thee.

3. There let the way appear
   Steps up to heaven ;
   All that thou sendest me,
   In mercy given,
   Angels to beckon me
   Nearer, my God, to thee,
   Nearer to thee.

4. Then with my waking thoughts,
   Bright with thy praise,
   Out of my stony griefs
   Bethel I'll raise ;

So by my woes to be
Nearer, my God, to thee.
Nearer to thee.

5. Or if on joyful wing
Cleaving the sky,
Sun, moon, and stars forgot,
Upward I fly.
Still all my song shall be,
Nearer, my God, to thee,
Nearer to thee.

---

## 186. Press On, Little Pilgrims.

1. PRESS on, little pilgrims,
And never give up,
Though often the desert is dreary;
Press on, little pilgrims,
Replenish your cup
From wells of salvation when weary.

CHORUS.

When you've crossed the river,
You'll be happy ever;
Safe on Canaan's shore,
You'll be happy ever more.

2. Press on, little pilgrims,
And lean on the Friend
Whose heart is the empire of pity;

Whose wisdom shall guide you,
Whose arm shall defend,
Till safe in the beautiful city.
CHORUS—When you 've crossed, etc.

3. Press on, little pilgrims,
And never retreat
When Satan comes forth to annoy you ;
The darts which he hurls
With a merciless hate,
May wound, but shall never destroy you.

4. Press on, little pilgrims,
Your home is in view ;
Its doors are thrown wide to receive you ;
A bright crown of glory
Is laid up for you,
And sorrow and sin shall soon leave you.

A. A. G.

## 187.  The Shining Way.

1. THE pearly gates are open wide,
I see the bright array ;
On either side the angels glide,
To keep the shining way.
And little children learn to find
The way by angels trod,
Where Christ's redeemed in union walk
The shining way of God.

CHORUS.

The pearly gates are open wide,
   I see the bright array ;
On either side the angels glide,
   To keep the shining way.

2. When storms arise, and darkness clouds
   The faithful pilgrims' way,
On either side the angels glide,
   To keep the shining way ;
And brighter gleams the morning light
   Behind the gentle rod,
For Christ's redeemed more clearly see
   The shining way of God.

3. And soon they walk the golden streets,
   Not slighted and alone ;
On either side the angels glide,
   To lead them to the throne :
And there they 'll wear a starry crown
   Who once did tire and plod,
For Christ's redeemed as kings shall tread
   The shining way of God.

## 188. The Pilgrim's Guide.

1. My Saviour, my almighty Friend,
   When I begin thy praise,
Where will the growing numbers end,
   The numbers of thy grace?

Thou art my everlasting trust,
  Thy goodness I adore ;
And since I knew thy graces first,
  I speak thy glories more.

2. My feet shall travel all the length
  Of the celestial road,
And march with courage in thy strength,
  To see my Father God.
When I am filled with sore distress
  For some surprising sin,
I 'll plead thy perfect righteousness,
  And mention none but thine.

3. How will my lips rejoice to tell
  The victories of my King ;
My soul redeemed from sin and hell,
  Shall thy salvation sing.
Awake, awake, my tuneful powers ;
  With this delightful song
I 'll entertain the darkest hours,
  Nor think the season long.    WATTS

## 189. Shall We Meet Beyond the River?

1. SHALL we meet beyond the river,
  Where the surges cease to roll,
Where, in all the bright for ever,
  Sorrow ne'er shall press the soul?
208

CHORUS.

Shall we meet, shall we meet,
Shall we meet, shall we meet,
Shall we meet beyond the river,
Where the surges cease to roll?

2. Shall we meet in that blest harbor
When our stormy voyage is o'er;
Shall we meet and cast the anchor
By the fair celestial shore?
CHORUS—Shall we meet, etc.

3. Where the music of the ransomed
Rolls in harmony around,
And creation swells the chorus
With its sweet melodious sound?
CHORUS—Shall we meet, etc.

4. Shall we meet with many a loved one,
Torn on earth from our embrace?
Shall we listen to their voices,
And behold them face to face?
CHORUS—Shall we' meet, etc.

5. Shall we meet with Christ our Saviour
When he comes to claim his own?
Shall we hear him bid us welcome,
And sit down upon his throne?
CHORUS—Shall we meet, etc.

HASTINGS.

## 190.  The Heavenly Land.

1. THERE's a land of peerless beauty,
     And of glory all untold,
   Where no shadow ever falleth,
     Where no sunny face grows old ;
   Where the crystal river floweth,
     With the tree upon its banks,
   And with love each bosom gloweth
     In the bright celestial ranks.

2. Oh to reach that clime of gladness,
     Be it all my soul's desire ;
   Whether joy be mine, or sadness,
     Upward still would I aspire.
   Brief the pang my heart that rendeth,
     Brief the joy that swells it here ;
   But the rapture never endeth
     Of that pure and blessed sphere.

3. There is Jesus, my Redeemer,
     With the many crowns he wears,
   And the scars of earthly wounding,
     Precious tokens which he bears ;
   There the angels, all so glorious,
     In the outer circle stand,
   While the souls by faith victorious
     Are a nearer, dearer band.

4. Then, while months and years are taking
   Like a dream their flight away,
If they bring me but the breaking
   Of the one eternal day,
. I will not regret their fleetness,
   Nor hold fast to things below,
I will only ask a meetness
   For the bliss to which I go.

A. D. SMITH, D. D.

## 191. Shall We Meet in Heaven?

1. SHALL we meet in heaven above,
   Shall we meet, shall we meet,
Shall we meet in heaven above,
   Meet in heaven above?
Yes, if we are justified
By the sacred crimson tide
Flowing from the Saviour's side,
   We shall meet in heaven.

2. Shall we wear the snowy robe,
   Shall we wear, shall we wear,
Shall we wear the snowy robe
   Worn by saints in heaven?
Yes, if we will onward press
In the way of holiness,
We shall wear the snowy dress
   Worn by saints in heaven.

3. Shall we strike the golden harp,
    Shall we strike, shall we strike,
  Shall we strike the golden harp,
    With the choir in heaven?
  Yes, if from the heart we sing
  Praises to our Saviour King,
  We shall strike the tuneful string
    With the choir in heaven.

4. Shall we wear a glorious crown,
    Shall we wear, shall we wear,
  Shall we wear a glorious crown
    On a throne in heaven?
  Yes, if we the conflict share,
  Every cross with patience bear,
  We that glorious crown shall wear
    On a throne in heaven.          A. A. G.

## 192.  The World Above.

1. HIGH above yon stars of night,
    Far away, far away,
  Floats a world, whose radiant light
    Never fades away.
  Who shall find admittance there?
  Who its boundless joy shall share?
  Who within its mansions fair
    Pass that endless day?

2. You and I may enter there
    If we will, if we will ;
Christ for us will homes prepare
    Free from every ill :
If we all our sins confess,
He 'll convey us by his grace,
Robed in his own righteousness,
    There with him to dwell.

## 193. Beautiful Land.

1. JERUSALEM, for ever bright,
    Beautiful land of rest.
No winter there, no chill of night—
    Beautiful land of rest!
The dripping cloud is chased away,
The sun breaks forth in endless day :
Jerusalem, the beautiful land of rest!
Jerusalem, the beautiful land of rest!

### CHORUS.

Beautiful land, beautiful land,
We wait impatient to behold
The gates of pearl, the streets of gold,
And nestle safe in Jesus' fold,
In the beautiful land,
The beautiful land of rest.

2. Jerusalem, for ever free,
   Beautiful land of rest,
   The soul's sweet home of liberty,
   Beautiful land of rest!
   The gyves of sin, the chains of woe,
   The ransomed there will never know.
   Jerusalem, the beautiful land of rest
   CHORUS—We wait impatient, etc.

3. Jerusalem, for ever dear,
   Beautiful land of rest,
   Thy pearly gates almost appear,          .
   Beautiful land of rest!
   And when we tread thy lovely shore,
   We'll sing the song we've sung before,
   Jerusalem, the beautiful land of rest!

## 194.  Asleep in Jesus.

1. ASLEEP in Jesus! blesséd sleep,
   From which none ever wake to weep,
   A calm and undisturbed repose,
   Unbroken by the last of foes.

2. Asleep in Jesus! Oh how sweet
   To be for such a slumber meet;
   With holy confidence to sing
   That death has lost its venomed sting.
   214

8. Asleep in Jesus! peaceful rest,
Whose waking is supremely blest;
No fear, no woe shall dim that hour
That manifests the Saviour's power.

4. Asleep in Jesus! Oh for me
May such a blissful refuge be :
Securely shall my ashes lie,
And wait the summons from on high.

### 195.  Home of the Blest.

1. OH when shall I dwell
In a mansion all bright,
And Jesus my Saviour behold ;
Or walk by his side
Like an angel of light,
In a city all garnished with gold?
CHORUS.
Home of the blest, home of the blest,
When wilt thou ever be mine!
Home of the blest, home of the blest,
Soon shalt thou ever be mine.

2. No pearl from the ocean,
No gold from the mine,
Can pardon and purity buy ;
I'll trust in the blood
Of a Saviour divine,
And I'll cling to his cross till I die.

3. Though light are the sorrows
   That burden a child,
And fleeting the tempest of woe,
   I long for the land
     That was never defiled ;
To the home of the blest would I go.

4. But while I'm a stranger
   Away from my home,
I'll toil in the vineyard and pray ;
   I'll carry the cross
     While I think of the crown,
And I'll watch for the break of the day.

A. A. G

## 196. Rest for the Weary.

1. In the Christian's home in glory,
   There remains a land of rest ;
There my Saviour's gone before me,
   To fulfil my soul's request.

CHORUS.

There is rest for the weary,
There is rest for the weary,
There is rest for the weary,
   There is rest for you.
On the other side of Jordan,
   In the sweet fields of Eden,
Where the tree of life is blooming,
   There is rest for you.

2. He is fitting up my mansion,
     Which eternally shall stand,
   For my stay shall not be transient
     In that holy, happy land.
          CHORUS—There is rest, etc.

3. Death itself shall then be vanquished,
     And its sting shall be withdrawn ;
   Shout for gladness, Oh ye ransomed,
     Hail with joy the rising morn.

---

### 197. The Eternal Home.

1. THIS is not my place of resting
     Mine's a city yet to come ;
   Onward to it I am hasting,
     On to my eternal home.
          CHORUS—There is rest, etc.

2. In it all is light and glory,
     O'er it shines a nightless day ;
   Every trace of sin's sad story,
     All the curse hath passed away.

3. There the Lamb our Shepherd leads us
     By the streams of life along,
   On the freshest pastures feeds us,
     Turns our sighing into song.

4. Soon we pass this desert dreary,
    Soon we bid farewell to pain ;
Never more are sad or weary,
    Never, never sin again.      BONAR.

## 198.  Rest in Christ.

1. COME, saith Jesus' sacred voice,
    Come and make my paths your choice ;
    I will guide you to your home ;
    Weary pilgrim, hither come.
      CHORUS—There is rest, etc.

2. Hither come, for here is found
    Balm for every bleeding wound,
    Peace which ever shall endure,
    Rest eternal, sacred, sure.

## 199.  Christ our Peace.

1. COME, ye sinners, poor and needy,
    Weak and wounded, sick and sore,
  Jesus ready stands to save you,
    Full of pity, love, and power.
      CHORUS—There is rest, etc. ·

2. Now, ye needy, come and welcome,
    God's free bounty glorify ;
  Faith he gives, and true repentance,
    Every grace that brings you nigh.
218      ·

3. Come, ye weary, heavy-laden,
    Bruised and mangled by the fall ;
If you tarry till you 're better,
    You will never come at all.

---

### 200. The Shining Shore.

1. My days are gliding swiftly by,
    And I, a pilgrim stranger,
Would not detain them as they fly,
    Those hours of toil and danger :

CHORUS.

For Oh, we stand on Jordan's strand,
    Our friends are passing over,
And just before, the shining shore
    We may almost discover.

2. We 'll gird our loins, my brethren dear,
    Our distant home discerning ;
Our absent Lord has left us word,
    Let every lamp be burning.
        CHORUS—For Oh, we stand, etc.

3. Should coming days be cold and dark,
    We need not cease our singing ;
That perfect rest naught can molest,
    Where golden harps are ringing.

4. Let sorrow's rudest tempest blow,
   Each chord on earth to sever,
   Our King says, "Come," and there's our home
   For ever, Oh, for ever.

---

### 201. The Sweetest Name.

1. THERE is no name so sweet on earth,
   No name so sweet in heaven,
   The name, before his wondrous birth,
   To Christ the Saviour given.

#### CHORUS.

We love to sing around our King,
And hail him "blessed Jesus;"
For there's no word ear ever heard,
So dear, so sweet as JESUS.

2. His human name they did proclaim,
   When Abram's Son they sealed him;
   The name that still, by God's good will,
   DELIVERER revealed him.
      CHORUS—We love to sing. etc.

3 And when he hung upon the tree,
   They wrote this name above him,
   That all might see the reason we
   For ever more must love him.

4. So now upon his Father's throne,
   Almighty to release us
From sins and pains, he gladly reigns
   The Prince and Saviour, JESUS.

---

### 202. The Strayed Lamb.

1. A GIDDY lamb, one afternoon,
   Had from the fold departed ;
The tender shepherd missed it soon,
   And sought it broken-hearted.
Not all the flock that shared his love
   Could from the search delay him,
Nor clouds of midnight darkness move,
   Nor fear of suffering stay him.

2. But night and day he went his way
   In sorrow till he found it ;
He saw it where it fainting lay,
   He clasped his arms around it ;
And closely sheltered in his breast,
   From every ill to save it,
He took it to his home of rest,
   And pitied and forgave it.

3. And thus the Saviour will receive
   The little ones who fear him ;
Their pains remove, their sins forgive,
   And draw them gently near him—

Blest while they live ; and when they die,
  When soul and body sever,
Conduct them to his home on high,
  To dwell with him for ever.

YOUNG REAPER.

### 203. Heavenly Mansions.

1. I SEE in heaven those mansions bright,
  The noonday sun outshining,
For those who feel the Saviour's love
  Around their hearts entwining.

CHORUS.

Oh, happy they who reach that place
  Where sorrow cometh never—
Who rest within his loving arms
  For ever and for ever.

2. If I could hear my Saviour say,
  " Thy sins are all forgiven ;"
Then I could see a shining house
  Awaiting me in heaven.
    CHORUS—Oh, happy they, etc.

3. Look how the children at his feet
  Their tiny crowns are flinging,
While angels on their downy wings
  The latest born are bringing.

222

4. Yes, I will love my Saviour now,
   And serve him in life's morning ;
For I can see the house on high
   Of his own hand's adorning.

------

### 204. We're Going Home.

1. YOUTHFUL pilgrims, whither bound
     Through this vale so fearful ?
   Passing o'er enchanted ground,
     Why are you so cheerful ?
   CHORUS.
   Oh we're going, going home
   To our happy, happy home.
To the city of our Saviour King,
     Where the golden crown they wear,
     And the palm of victory bear,
And they strike the golden harp as they sing.

2. Tell us why, when pleasure woos,
     You will not believe her ?
   Tell us why the heart you close
     On the gay deceiver ?
       CHORUS—Oh, we're going, etc.

3. When from ambush Satan's dart
     Wounds the pilgrim weary,
   Where's the balm to ease the smart
     In the desert dreary ?

4. But the deep cold river see,
   Pilgrims, just before you ;
   What will then your solace be
   When its waves roll o'er you ?

5. Pilgrims of the Saviour King,
   Earth's temptations scorning,
   We will join your band and sing
   In life's sunny morning.          A. A. G

## 205. A Father in the Promised Land.

1. I HAVE a Father in the promised land,
   I have a Father in the promised land,
   My Father calls me, I must go
   To meet him in the promised land.

### CHORUS.

I'll away, I'll away to the promised land,
I'll away, I'll away to the promised land,
My Father calls me, I must go
To meet him in the promised land.

2. I have a Saviour in the promised land,
   I have a Saviour in the promised land,
   My Saviour calls me, I must go
   To meet him in the promised land.
   CHORUS—I'll away, I'll away, etc.

3. I have a crown in the promised land,
   I have a crown in the promised land;
   When Jesus'calls me, I must go
   To wear it in the promised land.

4. I hope to meet you in the promised land
   I hope to meet you in the promised land
   At Jesus' feet, a joyous band,
   We'll praise him in the promised land.

## 206. Longing for Heaven.

1. YE angels who stand round the throne,
     And view my Immanuel's face,
   In rapturous songs make him known;
     Tune, tune your soft harps to his praise:
   He formed you the spirits you are,
     So happy, so noble, so good;
   When others sunk down in despair,
     Confirmed by his power ye stood.

2. Ye saints who stand nearer than they,
     And cast your bright crowns at his feet,
   His grace and his glory display,
     And all his rich mercy repeat
   He snatched you from hell and the grave,
     He ransomed from death and despair:
   For you he was mighty to save,
     Almighty to bring you safe there.

3. I want to put on my attire,
   Washed white in the blood of the Lamb;
I want to be one of your choir,
   And tune my sweet harp to his name:
I want, Oh I want to be there,
   Where sorrow and sin bid adieu,
Your joy and your friendship to share.
   To wonder and worship with you.
DE FLEURY.

## 207. The Sabbath.

1. How sweet is the Sabbath to me,
   The day when the Saviour arose;
'T is heaven his beauties to see,
   And in his soft arms to repose.
He knows I am weak and defiled,
   My life is but empty and vain;
But if he will make me his child,
   I 'll never forsake him again.

2. This day he invites me to come,
   How kindly he bids me draw near·
He offers me heaven for home,
   And wipes off the penitent tear:
He offers to pardon my sin,
   And keep me from every snare,
To sprinkle and cleanse me within,
   And show me his tenderest care.

## 208. Realms of the Blest.

1. WE speak of the realms of the blest,
   Of that country so bright and so fair,
And oft are its glories confessed;
   But what must it be to be there!
We speak of its pathway of gold,
   Of its walls decked with jewels, so rare,
Of its wonders and pleasures untold;
   But what must it be to be there!

2. We speak of its freedom from sin,
   From sorrow, temptation, and care,
From trials without and within;
   But what must it be to be there!
Do thou, Lord, 'midst gladness or woe,
   Still for heaven our spirits prepare,
And shortly we also shall know
   And feel what it is to be there.

## 209. I'm a Pilgrim.

1. I'M a pilgrim, and I'm a stranger;
   I can tarry, I can tarry but a'night.
Do not detain me, for I am going
   To where the fountains are ever flowing:
I'm a pilgrim, and I'm a stranger,
   I can tarry, I can tarry but a night.

227

2. There the glory is ever shining!
   O my longing heart, my longing heart is there
   Here in this country, so dark and dreary,
   I long have wandered, forlorn and weary.
   I 'm a pilgrim, and I 'm a stranger,
   I can tarry, I can tarry but a night.

3. There 's the city to which I journey ;
   My Redeemer, my Redeemer is its light!
   There is no sorrow, nor any sighing,
   Nor any sin there, nor any dying!
   I 'm a pilgrim, and I 'm a stranger,
   I can tarry, I can tarry but a night.

### 210.   Homeward Bound.

1. Out on an ocean all boundless we ride—
   We 're homeward bound, homeward bound .
   Tossed on the waves of a rough restless tide—
   We 're homeward bound, homeward bound.
   Far from the safe quiet harbor we 've rode,
   Seeking our Father's celestial abode,
   Promise of which on us each he bestowed—
   We 're homeward bound, homeward bound.

2. Wildly the storm sweeps us on as it roars—
   We 're homeward bound, homeward bound;
   Look, yonder lie the bright heavenly shores—
   We 're homeward bound, homeward bound.

Steady, O pilot, stand firm at the wheel ;
Steady, we soon shall outweather the gale :
Oh how we fly 'neath the loud creaking sail
    We 're homeward bound, homeward bound.

3 We 'll tell the world as we journey along,
    We 're homeward bound, homeward bound
Try to persuade them to enter our throng—
    We 're homeward bound, homeward bound.
Come, trembling sinner, forlorn and opprest,
Join in our number, Oh come and be blest ;
Journey with us to the mansions of rest—
    We 're homeward bound, homeward bound.

4. Into the harbor of heaven we glide—
    We 're home at last, home at last ;
Softly we drift on its bright silver tide—
    We 're home at last, home at last.
Glory to God, all our dangers are o'er,
We stand secure on the glorified shore ;
"Glory to God!" we will shout evermore ;
    We 're home at last, home at last!

## 211. Joyfully, Joyfully.

1. JOYFULLY, joyfully, onward we move,
Bound to the land of bright spirits above
Jesus our Saviour in mercy says, Come,
Joyfully, joyfully haste to your home.

Soon will our pilgrimage end here below,
Soon to the presence of God we shall go ;
Then if to Jesus our hearts have been given,
Joyfully, joyfully rest we in heaven.

2 Teachers and scholars have passed on before
Waiting, they watch us approaching the shore,
Singing to cheer us while passing along,
"Joyfully, joyfully haste to your home."
Sounds of sweet music there ravish the ear ;
Harps of the blessed, your strains we shall hear,
Filling with harmony heaven's high dome ;
Joyfully, joyfully, Jesus, we come.

3. Death with his arrow may soon lay us low ;
Safe in our Saviour, we fear not the blow :
Jesus hath broken the bars of the tomb ;
Joyfully, joyfully will we go home.
Bright will the morn of eternity dawn,
Death shall be conquered, his sceptre be gone
Over the plains of sweet Canaan we'll roam.
Joyfully, joyfully, safely at home.

## 212. The Lovely Land.

1. THERE is a land of pure delight,
  Where saints immortal reign ;
Infinite day excludes the night,
  And pleasures banish pain.

Oh the land, the lovely land,
  The land over Jordan's foam ;
On the golden strand
Wait the happy, happy band,
  To welcome the ransomed home.

2. There everlasting spring abides,
    And never-withering flowers :
  Death, like a narrow sea, divides
  This heavenly land from ours.
    CHORUS—Oh the land, etc.

3. Sweet fields, beyond the swelling flood,
    Stand dressed in living green ;
  So to the Jews old Canaan stood,
  While Jordan rolled between.
    CHORUS—Oh the land, etc.

4. Oh, could we make our doubts remove,
    Those gloomy doubts that rise,
  And view the Canaan that we love
  With unbeclouded eyes ;

5. Could we but climb where Moses stood,
    And view the landscape o'er,
  Not Jordan's stream nor death's cold flood
  Should fright us from the shore.

## 213. Beautiful Zion.

1. BEAUTIFUL Zion, built above,
Beautiful city that I love;
Beautiful gates of pearly white,
Beautiful temple, God its light.
He who was slain on Calvary,
Opens those pearly gates to me.
Zion, Zion, lovely Zion,
Beautiful Zion, city of our God.

2. Beautiful heaven, where all is light;
Beautiful angels, clothed in white;
Beautiful strains that never tire;
Beautiful harps through all the choir.
There shall I join the chorus sweet,
Worshipping at the Saviour's feet.
Zion, Zion, lovely Zion,
Beautiful Zion, city of our God.

3. Beautiful crowns on every brow,
Beautiful palms the conqueror's show:
Beautiful robes the ransomed wear,
Beautiful all who enter there.
Thither I press with eager feet;
There shall my rest be long and sweet.
Zion, Zion, lovely Zion,
Beautiful Zion, city of our God.

4. Beautiful throne for Christ our King,
Beautiful songs the angels sing ;
Beautiful rest—all wanderings cease ;
Beautiful home of perfect peace.
There shall my eyes the Saviour see ;
Haste to his heavenly home with me.
Zion, Zion, lovely Zion,
Beautiful Zion, city of our God.

---

## 214.  Sorrow is O'er.

1. WHAT to me are earth's pleasures,
And what its flowing tears?
What are all the sorrows I deplore?
There's a song ever swelling.
Still lingers on my ears,
"Oh, sorrow shall come again no more."

### CHORUS.

'T is a song from the home of the weary :
"Sorrow, sorrow is for ever o'er :
Happy now, ever happy
On Canaan's peaceful shore.
Oh, sorrow shall come again no more."

2. I seek not earthly glory,
Nor mingle with the gay ;
I desire not this world's gilded store :

There are voices now calling
From those bright realms of day,
"Oh, sorrow shall come again no more."
CHORUS—'T is a song, etc.

.3. 'T is a note that is wafted
Across the troubled wave;
'T is a song I've heard upon the shore;
'T is a sweet thrilling murmur
Around the Christian's grave:
"Oh, sorrow shall come again no more."
CHORUS—'T is a song, etc.

4. 'T is the loud-pealing anthem,
The victor's holy song,
Where the conflict and the strife are o'er;
When the saved ones for ever
In joyous notes prolong,
"Oh, sorrow shall come again no more."

———————

## 215. Welcome.

1. HAPPY shepherds in Judah,
That heard the angel host
Pouring out on earth the joy of heav'n;
But the chorals of angels
In silence all are lost,
When Jesus one word of love has given.

CHORUS.

'T is a voice from the brightness of glory ;
" Welcome, welcome to my home of joy :
Come to me all ye weary, ye heavy-laden, come ,
I 'll give you a rest without alloy."

2. He is Lord of earth and heaven,
    And his almighty power
Can redeem from Satan and from hell ;
    He can hush Sinai's thunder,
    And in the final hour
Can take us with him in bliss to dwell.
    CHORUS—'T is a voice, etc.

3. Let us hear then our Saviour,
    Whatever be his word,
And his lightest whisper well obey ;
    That in peril and sorrow
    We still may hear our Lord
Bid our sorrows and perils flee away.
    CHORUS—'T is a voice, etc.

--------

### 216.  No Sorrow There.

1. OH sing to me of heaven
    When I am called to die ;
Sing songs of holy ecstacy
    To waft my soul on high.

CHORUS.

There 'll be no sorrow there,
There 'll be no sorrow there ;
In heaven above, where all is love,
There 'll be no sorrow there.

2. When cold and sluggish drops
   Roll off my marble brow,
Break forth in songs of joyfulness ;
   Let heaven begin below.
     CHORUS—There'll be no sorrow, etc.

3. Then to my raptured ear
   Let one sweet song be given ;
Let music charm me last on earth,
   And greet me first in heaven.

4. When round my senseless clay
   Assemble those I love,
Then sing of heaven, delightful heaven,
   My glorious home above.

## 217. Evening Hymn.

1. THE day is past and gone,
   The evening shades appear ;
Oh may we all remember well
   The night of death draws near.

2. Lord, keep us safe this night
   Secure from all our fears ;
   May angels guard us while we sleep,
   Till morning light appears.

3. And when we early rise,
   And view the unwearied sun,
   May we set out to win the prize,
   And after glory run.

4. And when our days are past,
   And we from time remove,
   Oh may we in thy bosom rest,
   The bosom of thy love.

---

## 218. A Crown of Glory Bright.

1. A CROWN of glory bright
   By faith I see,
   In yonder realms of light,
   Prepared for me.

CHORUS.

I 'm nearer my home, nearer my home,
Nearer my home to-day ;
Yes, nearer my home in heaven to-day
Than ever I 've been before.

237

2. Oh may I faithful prove,
   The crown in view,
And through the storms of life
   My way pursue.

3. Jesus, be thou my guide,
   My steps attend;
Oh keep me near thy side;
   Be thou my friend.

4. Be thou my shield and sun,
   My guide and guard;
And when my work is done,
   My great reward.

### 219. Little Travellers.

1. LITTLE travellers Zionward,
   Each one entering into rest,
In the kingdom of your Lord,
   In the mansions of the blest;
There to welcome Jesus waits,
   Gives the crown his followers win;
Lift your heads, ye golden gates,
   Let the little travellers in.

2. Who are they whose little feet,
   Pacing life's dark journey through,
Now have reached that heavenly seat
   They had ever kept in view?

I, from Greenland's frozen land ;"
"I, from India's sultry plain ;"
"I, from Afric's barren sand ;"
"I, from islands of the main."

4. "All our earthly journey passed,
Every tear and pain gone by,
Here together met at last
At the portal of the sky,
Each the welcome 'Come' awaits,
Conquerors over death and sin."
Lift your heads, ye golden gates,
Let the little travellers in.

## 220. Beautiful River.

1. SHALL we gather at the river,
Where bright angel feet have trod ;
With its crystal tide for ever
Flowing by the throne of God?

CHORUS.

Yes, we'll gather at the river,
The beautiful, the beautiful river—
Gather with the saints at the river
That flows by the throne of God.

2. On the margin of the river,
Washing up its silver spray,
We will walk and worship ever,
All the happy, golden day.

239

3. Ere we reach the shining river,
    Lay we every burden down ;
  Grace our spirits will deliver,
    And provide a robe and crown.

4. At the smiling of the river,
    Mirror of the Saviour's face,
  Saints whom death will never sever,
    Lift their songs of saving grace.

5. Soon we 'll reach the silver river,
    Soon our pilgrimage will cease ;
  Soon our happy hearts will quiver
    With the melody of peace.

## 221.    Roll, Jordan, Roll.

1. ROLL, Jordan, roll,
  Thy foaming waters roll along ;
No ill I fear, for Christ is near,
  His rod and staff are strong :
My Lord will meet me on the shore,
  When heart and flesh shall fail ;
His presence dear my soul will cheer
When deep in Jordan's vale.

CHORUS.

Oh swiftly the Jordan rolls,
  Its billows are dashing on the shore ;
He 'll bid the tide abase its pride,
  And bring me safely o'er.

2. Roll, Jordan, roll,
Thy foaming waters roll along;
Beyond thee lies fair Paradise,
Where Christ's redeemed belong.
Though sin and Satan join their power
To plunge me in the deep,
The raging foe cannot o'erthrow
The soul that Christ doth keep.
Chorus—Oh swiftly the Jordan, etc.

3. Roll, Jordan, roll,
Thy foaming waters roll along;
The hosts of God thy bed have trod
With trumpet and with song:
Right through thy waves with pomp divine
The fiery pillar passed,
In days of yore, and brought them o'er
To Canaan's land at last.
Chorus—Oh swiftly the Jordan, etc.

4. Roll. Jordan, roll,
Thy foaming waters roll along;
Both young and old thy billows cold
Await—an endless throng.
Through fear of death though tremblers lie
In bondage all their life,
My soul aspires with warm desires
In thee to end its strife.
Chorus—Oh swiftly the Jordan, etc.

16      241

## 222. The Heaven Above.

1. THERE 's a bright, unfading crown
    In the heaven above,
Sparkling like the dews of morn,
    In the heaven above.
Thousands of children there
That crown of glory wear,
Now safe from sin and care,
    In the heaven above.

2. There 's a robe of righteousness
    In the heaven above ;
Worn by every heir of grace,
    In the heaven above ;
Happy and undefiled,
Many a ransomed child,
Shines like the starlight mild,
    In the heaven above.

3. There 's a tuneful harp of gold
    In the heaven above ;
Every hand a harp shall hold
    In the heaven above.
Thousands of children sing
Praise to their Saviour King ;
Loud sweep the tuneful string
    In the heaven above.

4. Would you strike that golden wire
    In the heaven above—
Wear that crown and that attire
    In the heaven above?
Come then to Jesus, come ;
Come in your youthful bloom ;
Come, for there now is room
    In the heaven above.　　　A. A. G

---

## 223. Sabbath Eve.

1. How sweet the light of Sabbath eve,
    How soft the sunbeams lingering there :
For these blest hours the world I leave,
    Wafted on wings of praise and prayer.

2. The time how lovely and how still !
    Peace shines and smiles on all below ;
The plain, the stream, the wood, the hill,
    All fair with evening's setting glow.

3. Season of rest ! the tranquil soul ·
    Feels the sweet calm, and melts to love
And while these sacred moments roll,
    Faith sees a smiling heaven above.

4. Nor will our days of toil be long,
    Our pilgrimage will soon be trod
And we shall join the ceaseless song,
    The endless Sabbath of our God. EDMESTON.

## 224. Abide With Me.

1. Sun of my soul, thou Saviour dear,
   It is not night if thou be near :
   Oh may no earth-born cloud arise
   To hide thee from thy servant's eyes.

2. When soft the dews of kindly sleep
   My wearied eyelids gently steep,
   Be my last thought—how sweet to rest
   For ever on my Saviour's breast.

3. Abide with me from morn till eve,
   For without thee I cannot live ;
   Abide with me when night is nigh,
   For without thee I dare not die.

4. Be near to bless me when I wake,
   Ere through the world my way I take ,
   Abide with me till in thy love
   I lose myself in heaven above.     KEBLE.

## 225. Sabbath Eve.

1. Thine earthly Sabbaths, Lord, we love,
   But there's a nobler rest above :
   To that our longing souls aspire,
   With ardent love and strong desire.

244

2. No more fatigue, no more distress,
  Nor sin nor death shall reach the place ;
  No groans shall mingle with the songs
  Which warble from immortal tongues.

3. No rude alarms of raging foes ;
  No cares to break the long repose ;
  No midnight shade, no clouded sun,
  But sacred, high, eternal noon.

4. Oh, long expected day, begin !
  Dawn on this world of woe and sin ;
  Fain would we leave this weary road,
  To sleep in death and rest in God.

DODDRIDGE

## 226. Daily Devotion.

1. My God, how endless is thy love ;
  Thy gifts are every evening new ;
  And morning mercies from above
  Gently distil like early dew.

2. Thou spreadest the curtains of the night,
  Great Guardian of my sleeping hours ;
  Thy sovereign word restores the light,
  And quickens all my drowsy powers.

3. I yield my powers to thy command,
  To thee I consecrate my days ;
  Perpetual blessings from thy hand
  Demand perpetual songs of praise. WATTS

## 227. The Heavenly Mansion.

1. My heavenly home is bright and fair,
Nor pain nor death can enter there ;
Its glittering towers the sun outshine ;
That heavenly mansion shall be mine.

2. My Father's house is built on high,
Far, far above the starry sky :
When from this earthly prison free,
That heavenly mansion mine shall be.

3. Let others seek a home below,
Which flames devour, or waves o'erflow ;
Be mine the happier lot—to own
A heavenly mansion near the throne.

4. Then fail this earth, let stars decline,
And sun and moon refuse to shine,
All nature sink and cease to be ;
That heavenly mansion stands for me.

## 228. Evening Hymn.

1. GLORY to thee, my God, this night,
For all the blessings of the light :
Keep me, Oh keep me, King of kings,
Beneath the shadow of thy wings.

2. Forgive me, Lord, through thy dear Son,
The ills which I this day have done ;
That with the world, myself, and thee,
I, ere I sleep, at peace may be.

3. Teach me to live, that I may dread
The grave as little as my bed ;
Teach me to die, that so I may
Rise glorious at the judgment-day.

4. Praise God, from whom all blessings flow ;
Praise him, all creatures here below ;
Praise him above, ye heavenly host ;
Praise Father, Son, and Holy Ghost.  KENX.

---

## 229. Going to Christ.

1. JESUS, my all, to heaven is gone,
He whom I fix my hopes upon ;
His track I see, and I'll pursue
The narrow way till him I view.

2. So glad I come, and thou, blest Lamb,
Shall take me to thee as I am :
Nothing but sin I thee can give,
Nothing but love shall I receive.

3 Then will I tell to sinners round
What a dear Saviour I have found ;
I'll point to thy redeeming blood,
And say, Behold the way to God!

## 230. Morning Hymn.

1. GOD of the morning, at whose voice
   The cheerful sun makes haste to rise,
   And like a giant doth rejoice
   To run his journey through the skies:

2. Oh, like the sun, may I fulfil
   The appointed duties of the day;
   With ready mind and active will
   March on and keep my heavenly way.

3. But I shall rove and lose the race,
   If God, my sun, should disappear,
   And leave me in this world's wild maze
   To follow every wandering star.

4. Give me thy counsel for my guide,
   And then receive me to thy bliss;
   All my desires and hopes beside
   Are faint and cold compared with this.

WATTS.

## 231. The Beautiful World.

1. THERE 's beauty in the sunshine,
   There 's beauty in the showers;
   There 's beauty in the wildwood,
   There 's beauty in the flowers:

The valley and the mountain,
　The ocean and the plain,
In beauty robed, entrance the heart,
　And every sense enchain.

### CHORUS.

Beautiful world, beautiful world, beautiful, beau-
　tiful world ;
Beautiful world, beautiful world, beautiful, beau-
　tiful world.

2. But there's a world above us
　　More beautiful and pure,
Where all that's bright and lovely
　　For ever shall endure :
No angry storms assail it,
　　No blast nor sickly blight,
No chilling winds, no burning heats,
　　No dark and dreary night.
　　Chorus—Beautiful world, etc.

3. We weep, for here we languish,
　　But there's no sorrow there ;
The eye that fondly gazes
　　Shall never shed the tear :
No pangs of sad bereavement
　　Shall pierce the mourner's heart,
No grassy grave shall mar the ground,
　　No death shall hurl the dart.

4. One season bland and vernal
   Shall bless that hallowed ground,
And changeless and eternal
   Shall beauty smile around :
From hunger, thirst, and weakness
   The ransomed souls are free ;
They drink the stream, they pluck the fruit
   Of immortality.

## 232. Sunlight.

1. THE sun shines bright,
   And it pours its light
O'er the valley, the field, and flood ;
   The night-bird flies
   From the sunlit skies,
To his home in the leafy wood.

CHORUS.

Then sleep no more, for the day is come,
   The night with its gloom has fled ;
With a cheerful heart fulfil your part,
   And the path of duty tread.

2. God's word is light,
   Like the sun so bright,
And it shines in this Christian clime ;
   And sin retires
   From its searching fires,
To its home in the dens of crime.

250

3. Poor pagans sleep
   In their gloom so deep,
Not a star lends its feeble ray ;
   But rays divine
   On your pathway shine,
And you bask in the bright broad day.


4. Then pray and toil
   For a little while,
And the wants of the world supply ;
   Do all you can,
   Whether child or man,
For the night of the grave draws nigh.

A. A. G.

---

### 233. Away to the Woods.

1. Away to the woods, away,
   Away to the woods, away ;
   All nature is smiling,
   Our young hearts beguiling,
   Oh we will be happy to-day.

CHORUS.

||:Away, away, away, away,
   Away to the woods, away, :||
||:Away to the woods, away to the woods,
   Away to the woods, away ;:||

2. Our flag to the breezes fling,
   Our flag to the breezes fling,
   And as it waves o'er us,
   We'll join in the chorus,
   Till woodland and valley shall ring.
     CHORUS—Away, away, etc.

3. Oh this is our festal day,
   Oh this is our festal day;
   Sweet flowerets are springing,
   Sweet songsters are singing,
   And we will be happy and gay.

4. As free as the air are we,
   As free as the air are we;
   Then rally, then rally,
   From hill-top and valley,
   And join in our innocent glee.

5. We all of us love the school,
   We all of us love the school;
   And 't is in well-doing
   We're pleasure pursuing,
   For truth is our guide and our rule.

6. Success to the school we love,
   Success to the school we love;
   It sweetens employment
   With harmless enjoyment,
   And trains for the kingdom above. a

## 234. Come where the Wild Flowers Grow.

1. Come where the wild flowers grow,
   By the gushing fountain ;
   Come where the zephyrs blow
   Over plain and mountain ;
   Come where the streamlets dance,
   Light as sportive childhood ;
   Come where the sunbeams dance
   Through the shady wildwood.

2. Come where the violets blue
   Rich perfumes are breathing,
   Come where the sunny brow
   Roses red are wreathing :
   Sweet sing the feathered choir,
   Not a note of sadness
   Falls on the ravished ear ;
   All is glee and gladness.

3. Come when the placid wave
   Glows in sunset glory ;
   Come when the dewy eve
   Veils the mountain hoary ;
   Come when the rustic hearth
   Gathers youth and beauty ;
   Come, and with gentle mirth
   Sweeten toil and duty.            A A 3.

## 235. Land of the Free.

1. My country, my country,
      I cherish thee still,
Though many the ills that defile thee :
      I 'll weep o'er thy woe,
        And I 'll pray for thy weal,
And never, no, never revile thee.

**CHORUS.**

||:Land of the free,
   Land of the free,
   Bright burns the flame
   Of devotion to thee!:||

2. I 've drunk of the cup
      Which thy bounty supplied,
When peace with her olive-wreath crowned
        thee;
      And when thou art tossing
      On war's stormy tide,
My heart shall cling closer around thee.
      CHORUS—Land of the free, etc.

3. The traitor at home,
      And the foeman abroad,
May league to divide and enslave thee ;
      But He who of old
      Was thy guide and thy guard,
Will watch o'er the greatness he gave thee.

4. Here justice shall reign,
    And the bondsman shall sing
Farewell to his tears and his anguish ;
    For under the eagle
    Of liberty's wing
No child of oppression shall languish.


5. 'T is Liberty's prayer,
    'T is Humanity's plea,
"Be palsied the hand that would sever
    The land of the brave
    And the land of the free ;
The Union, the Union for ever.    A. A. G.

---

### 236. America.

1. My country, 't is of thee,
    Sweet land of liberty,
      Of thee I sing ;
    Land where my fathers died,
    Land of the pilgrims' pride,
    From every mountain side
      Let "Freedom" ring.

2. My native country, thee,
    Land of the noble free,
      Thy name I love ;

## 239. Sing Jesus' Name.

1. COME and join our happy song,
Evermore sing Jesus' name :
Heart and voice to him belong,
Evermore sing Jesus' name.

CHORUS.

Oh, love Jesus ;
Oh, bless Jesus ; •
Oh, praise Jesus ;
Evermore sing Jesus' name.

2. Sing of him from heaven who **came,**
Evermore sing Jesus' name—
The song of Moses and the Lamb ;
Evermore sing Jesus' name.
CHORUS—Oh, love Jesus, etc.

3. Jesus' name can save us all,
Evermore sing Jesus' name ;
Jesus bids us on him call,
Evermore sing Jesus' name.

4. Those that love him he will bless--
Evermore sing Jesus' name ;
Clothe them with his righteousness,
Evermore sing Jesus' name.

5. Oh. that all would love our Lord,
      Evermore sing Jesus' name ;
   Trust his grace, and keep his word,
      Evermore sing Jesus' name.

6. And in heaven at length may we
      Evermore sing Jesus' name ;
   Praise him through eternity,
      Evermore sing Jesus' name.

------·------

## 240. Morning Prayer.

1. Our Father in heaven,
      We hallow thy name ;
   May thy kingdom holy
      On earth be the same ;
   Oh, give to us daily
      Our portion of bread,
   For 't is from thy bounty
      That all must be fed.

2. Forgive our transgressions,
      And teach us to know
   That humble compassion
      That pardons each foe ;
   Keep us from temptation,
      From weakness, and sin,
   And thine be the glory
      For ever, Amen.

## 241.  Ministering Angels.

1. How cheering the thought
That the spirits in bliss
Should bow their bright wings
To a world such as this,
And leave the sweet songs
Of the mansions above,
To breathe o'er our bosoms
Some message of love.

2. They come! on the wings
Of the morning they come,
The pilgrim to waft
From this stormy abode—
To convoy the stranger
In peace to his home,
And lay him to rest
In the arms of his God.

## 242.  Evening Prayer.

1. Jesus, tender Shepherd, hear us ;
Bless thy little lambs to-night ;
Through the darkness be thou near us ;
Keep us safe till morning light.

2. All this day thy hand has led us,
   And we thank thee for thy care ;
   Thou hast clothed us, warmed us, fed us,
   Listen to our evening prayer.

3. May our sins be all forgiven ;
    Bless the friends we love so well ;
   Take us, when we die, to heaven.
   Happy there with thee to dwell.

DUNCAN

## 243. Parting Hymn.

1. HAPPILY we have met around our King,
   Words of life to hear, his praise to sing.
   Friendly hands to grasp, while eye to eye
   Flashes out the spark of love and joy.
   Happy, happy moments, all too soon you're gone,
   And the time of parting comes swiftly flying on:

CHORUS.
   Lift we then yet once again
   A happy song of praise,
   Once again a loving eye
   To our Redeemer raise,
   Beg of him upon each head
   His hand of love to lay,
   Giving each a work, a smile,
   A blessing on our way.

261

So shall He guide us
Till partings are o'er,
||:And welcome us all
On eternity's shore. :||

2. Cheerily we have met as voyagers meet,
Sailing on their way to friends and home ;
Or as at a fount of waters sweet
Travellers who o'er the desert roam ;
Hours of sweet refreshment, girding up the soul,
Eagerly to hasten towards the heavenly goal :
CHORUS—Lift we then yet once, etc.

3. Joyfully we have met in Jesus' name,
Hopefully we part beneath his care,
Seeking how we may his love proclaim,
Bringing all we can that love to share ;
Brighter thus each day shall rise our pilgrim sun
Larger still our numbers the joyful race to run.

------

## 244. O Come, let Us Sing. Chant.

1. O COME, let us sing un- | to the | Lord ; |
Let us heartily rejoice in the | strength of :
our sal- | vation.
Let us come before his presence | with thanks
| giving, |
And show ourselves | glad in | him with
psalms.

2. For the Lord is a | great— | God ;
And a great | King a- | bove all | gods.
In his hand are all the corners | of the | earth;
And the strength of the | hills is | his— | also.

3 The sea is his, | and he | made it ;
And his hands pre- | pared—the | dry | land.
O come, let us worship | and fall | down,
And kneel be- | fore the | Lord our | Maker.

4. For he is the | Lord our | God ;
And we are the people of his pasture, and
the | sheep of | his— | hand.
O worship the Lord in the | beauty.. of | holi-
ness ;
Let the whole earth | stand in | awe of | him.

5. For he cometh, for he cometh to | judge the |
earth ;
And with righteousness to judge the world,
and the | people | with his | truth.

6. Glory be to the Father, and | to the | Son,
And | to the | Holy | Ghost ;
As it was in the beginning, is now, and ever
| shall be,
World | without . end.  A- | men.

# INDEX OF HYMNS.

# INDEX OF HYMNS.

# INDEX OF HYMNS.

# INDEX OF HYMNS.

# INDEX OF HYMNS.

268

# INDEX OF HYMNS.

# INDEX OF HYMNS.